I hope you find this helpful in focusing you in on doing less, better.

Crawford

What People Are Saying about *Live Free or DIY*

"Do you feel drained by your own business? Are you sensing things can be done better or more efficiently? Running your own business should continually provide you renewed energy. Live Free or DIY *is a game changer in this arena. In this book, Justin explains that being a "DIYer" is what's holding you back from true success. Follow along, and* ***make some changes****. You'll see the results you've been dreaming of."*

—Ashish Patil
Serial Entrepreneur & Product Specialist,
DesignedGrowth.com

"Justin's Efficiency Roadmap process outlines clear and easy steps to achieve new levels of success in your business. This manual is essential for every small business owner, and brilliantly applies Justin's expertise in practical and powerful ways."

—Matt Steinruck
Founder & CEO, Big Picture Studio

"Being a small business owner, I can relate to the dilemma of finding the work-life-family balance all business owners only dream about. Justin has given me a guide to help me navigate the blue waters of my business. Thanks Justin, without this guide, my business would be like cereal without the milk!!"

—Claudia Guzman
CEO of Global Assist

"From managing time to growing a customer base to dealing with taxes and regulations, Live Free or DIY *will show you how to turn your biggest problems into your newest competitive advantage. You'll only wish you read it sooner."*

—Todd Lochner

Author and President of Lochner Law Firm, P.C.

"Avoid the common mistakes of a first time entrepreneur. A few hours of understanding these concepts will truly help you focus your precious resources."

—Troy Lawson

Inventor, Technologist, and Former C-Level Executive turned Consultant

"The breadth and clarity of the information makes Live Free or DIY *an invaluable tool. At the top of the long list of thought provoking concepts is the Golden Formula which helps us calculate the value of how we spend our time. This was a real eye opener for me, showing me where I really needed to make significant changes. From time management tools to tips on how to more effectively strategize your business, I found value in every chapter. Justin has lived what he writes about and I'm grateful he has chosen to share his experience with us!"*

—Claire Brown Kohler

Founder, We Empower Leaders

LIVE FREE OR DIY

HOW TO GET MORE CUSTOMERS,

FREE

INCREASE PROFITS,

AND ACHIEVE WORK-LIFE BALANCE

JUSTIN E. CRAWFORD

Published in the United States by Redwood Digital Publishing. Books are available at special discounts when purchased in bulk for sales promotions or corporate use. For more information, please write: info@redwooddigitalpublishing.com and include the title of the book in the email subject line.

Printed in the United States of America

ISBN Hardcover: 978-0-692-67123-8
ISBN Paperback: 978-0-692-68952-3
ISBN eBook: 978-0-692-67122-1

Library of Congress Control Number: 2016937090

Cover Design: Michelle Manley
Interior Design: Ghislain Viau

TABLE OF CONTENTS

PART I

How DIY Is Drowning Your Business

PART II

A New Road Map For Effective Small-Business Operations

PART III

Automate the Boring Stuff, Because Passion Produces Profit

PART IV

Practical Answers to the Questions Small-Business Owners Are Asking

PART I

How DIY Is Drowning Your Business

The chief problem facing most small-business owners is not a lack of effort, will, or talent. Instead, the problem is time and resource management. It's a question of figuring out how to do the right things at the right times with the right resources. And that's a tricky balance—especially because the most effective strategies are sometimes counterintuitive.

Part I of this book will turn the prevailing wisdom on its head to show why DIYing isn't just a bad idea, but how it could squash your otherwise promising business. It will also introduce some key alternative strategies to set you on the path to success.

In this section you'll find:

1. Why your time is more valuable than your money.
2. Why confusing *cheap* and *efficient* will cost you big.
3. How to tap into the start-up capital you never knew you had.
4. How to use the Golden Formula for maximizing the value of your time.
5. How to build a team of experts—on a shoestring budget—to achieve more than your business ever could have before.

1

The Million-Dollar Calculator: Money Matters, but Time Drives Your Bottom Line

So often people are working hard at the wrong thing. Working on the right thing is probably more important than working hard.

—Caterina Fake (Founder, Flickr)

Maybe you can remember the precise moment the idea came to you. It was an ordinary day—just another day when you were working at that tiresome job and watching someone else reap the reward for your hard work. Then it hit you. The entrepreneurial jolt: *You would start your own business!*

After all, people had been telling you for a long time that you're great at what you do. And you *are* great at what you do, perhaps most of all because you love doing it. So when the idea hit you to start your own business, you knew it was the right thing. You also wanted the chance to become your own boss, make your own schedule, and achieve financial freedom.

So you summoned your courage—and your savings—and you charged boldly forward. Immediately, though, that meant you had to incorporate the business and set up a bank account and perhaps a credit line. Soon you had your first customers, and you realized you needed a bookkeeping system. Plus, since most of your potential customers had never heard of you, you had to figure out how to get your name out there. That meant you'd need some kind of marketing plan. All of this was like the Wild West: You started your own business because you're an expert at what you do, not because you knew the nitty-gritty of small-business operations.

But you're smart, so you knew you could learn how to do accounting, set up a website, and develop a marketing plan, not to mention hire employees and supervise them, manage payroll, and stay on top of labor regulations, in addition to the seemingly endless stream of other tasks that came your way.

"I'll figure it out," you thought to yourself. "I'm an entrepreneur, after all!"

And so you kept charging forward.

A year passed, and then two. You found yourself working around the clock week in, week out. And you had a feeling you weren't making much money, though you weren't precisely sure, since the answer was buried in those account books that you never seem to have the time to balance.

And it was at the end of yet another grueling week, when you came home late on a Saturday night and collapsed on the couch, that you began to wonder if there was a better way.

The Million-Dollar Calculator

I've worked with a lot of small-business owners, and the story you just read describes entrepreneurs in every industry, from small-town pizza shops to lawyers running their own firms to tech wizards launching new-media platforms. Besides working themselves to exhaustion and feeling unsatisfied with the results, what do all these entrepreneurs have in common?

They're all trying to build a million-dollar calculator.

Think for a moment about a little plastic calculator. You can pick one up at the dollar store for pennies. Now imagine that, instead of obtaining a calculator by buying one (or downloading an app onto your phone), you decide the only way is to *build it yourself*.

You assemble plastic and wires and metal and rare earth minerals, not to mention the ingredients to build a battery too. But you soon discover that the process is frustrating and may take years—nay, decades—for you to build this little calculator all by yourself. And as you wade further and further into the process, you realize all the time and materials and know-how required to build this calculator will cost you far more than you imagined. When it's all said and done, it's probably going to cost you a million dollars.

If everyone who needed a calculator—or a computer, or a car, or a piece of clothing, or a pair of shoes, or anything else—took the approach of trying to build it from scratch, our entire global economy would grind to a halt. Despite having built automobiles for most of a century, Toyota wouldn't be able to sell another car. Apple wouldn't sell another computer. Your favorite neighborhood takeout joint wouldn't sell one more meal. And meanwhile, everyone's life quality would plummet, because no one would benefit from anyone else's expertise.

Yet the vast majority of entrepreneurs—a group that includes brilliant doctors setting up their own practices and bright young attorneys starting out on their own, not to mention masters at the art of making mouthwatering pizza or photo-worthy cappuccino—attempts the equivalent of building that million-dollar calculator by trying to DIY every piece of their business.

You're Not Alone

Depending on how you do the counting, between 13 and 20 percent of U.S. adults are involved in start-ups or newly established businesses, according to research reported in Forbes.[1]

That means you're not alone in this battle, though it can feel like a lonely journey. In fact, there are numerous resources out there to help you, resources that draw on the deep expertise of the many entrepreneurs who've walked the same road.

Of course, you'd probably be the first to admit you're not capable of building a calculator from scratch (few human beings are!). On the other hand, you *are* capable of learning basic accounting, and basic marketing, and how to deal with payroll, and—more or less—how to keep your business from violating major labor laws and other relevant regulations, and a lengthy list of other things with which you've now got to deal. But the question isn't whether you're *capable* of doing all these things, it's whether you *should* do them: **Are you helping your business by becoming a jack-of-all-trades instead of focusing on what you do best?**

The answer, which runs counter to the way the vast majority of entrepreneurs operate, is *no.*

When they hear me say that for the first time, a lot of business owners respond with a list of "buts":

- *But I* have *to do these things myself because I can't afford to hire someone.*
- *But it would take more time to train someone than to just do it myself!*
- *But I've already learned how to do all this stuff, so I might as well keep doing it.*
- *But no one else cares about my business like I do.*

The list goes on, but the "buts" stop here. In the pages ahead we're going to address each of these issues and many, many more. We're going to do so by focusing on the single most valuable resource available to you and your business. It's the ultimate *non-*renewable resource: your time.

What do international shipping and small-town law have in common?

I discovered a better, faster, more efficient and cost-effective way for businesses to operate while I was working in the strange world of international shipping. Then I discovered it all over again when I left international shipping to set up shop as a lawyer.

If that sounds like a strange path to get to where I am now—at the helm of a company that's changing the way small businesses operate—it is, but it's also given me a chance to study businesses large and small, hyper local to completely global. I've collaborated with entrepreneurs delivering products as varied as bottled liquor, virtual networking, legal counsel, and consumer-goods containers the size of highway tractor-trailers.

A number of years back I founded a marine-operations business. The idea was to manage international shipping on a contract basis for a big company, which meant that I was entering a vast, multibillion-dollar industry in which margins were razor-thin.

Just to give you a quick glimpse into this crazy world, consider this: A T-shirt priced at $12 in your nearest department store has probably traveled twenty thousand miles aboard various container ships while making its journey from raw cotton to retail product. But how much does the shipping company earn for moving that shirt across all those miles—halfway around the world and back? About ten cents. Needless to say, efficiency is the name of this particular game.

And it probably looked crazy at the time, but I thought I saw a way to improve efficiency in an industry that was already devoting billions of dollars to shaving pennies from its cost structure in order to stay competitive. I believed I could do things better than they were being done, and thus raise profits—while also carving out some profits for myself.

Fortunately, one of the ten largest global container-shipping companies in the world was crazy enough to take a chance on my little experiment. So with that big-time contract secured, my little company was officially responsible for managing marine activity in North, South, and Central America east of the Panama Canal for one of the biggest container-shipping companies in the world.

Working Smart vs. Working Hard

According to research done by Stanford University, overwork actually leads to decreased output.[2] *That is, total output from, say, a sixty-hour workweek, is frequently less than total output from a forty-hour workweek*—even though it contains 50 percent more working hours!

Why? Your average productivity can drop by 35 percent or more when you're overworked. Meanwhile, mistakes made in those late hours—when you're pushing yourself too hard—can offset the extra time worked by requiring you to spend time correcting errors. Either way, the point is clear: Working smart is more important than working hard.

Was I intimidated? You bet. Did I feel like I really knew the ins and outs of running a business? Absolutely not.

But here's what I did know.

Before starting my company, I'd spent a few years working in the shipping industry, and I'd noticed that some of the standard industry practices made no sense at all. Employees were expected to sit in a cubicle at regional headquarters from eight o'clock in the morning to six o'clock in the evening, Monday through Friday, *and* be on call 24/7/365. Since the very essence of the business was managing ships out on the open sea, the work couldn't stop for weekends or holidays or anything else. And far too much of what we did—making stowage plans for vessels after loading figures came in at six o'clock, or handling emergency problems on board a ship—were outside the eight-to-six workday. That meant that during the workweek itself, we showed up just to show up. We were in our cubicles during the required hours, though we didn't actually have a lot to do.

So the first thing I changed when I started my own business was the schedule. I knew that, in my industry, eight-to-six office hours were a waste of time.

I also knew most of the jobs in marine operations paid a healthy, often six-figure, salary. That was the case even though those workers spent just a few hours a week on the really important stuff, like three-o'clock-in-the-morning phone calls for bringing a ship into port, resolving some onboard crisis, or making a decision that would affect millions of dollars of cargo. The rest of their time was more or less spent creating reports, sending e-mails about scheduling, or doing nothing at all during that eight-to-six workday.

I saw a different way. Why pay a highly skilled shipping expert to work full-time when you really only need his or her expertise ten hours a week? I could pay an expert for part-time work, and then train someone at $15 or $20 per hour to handle e-mail and other clerical tasks.

So that's precisely what I did. A tweak to the workflow, plus some investments in the latest technology and a serious rethinking of where and how everyone worked, and I had myself an operating plan. And what happened?

My profits soared while, at the same time, I *saved* big money for my client.

What's more, as my business grew and I hired more employees, I discovered that I had my pick of the best talent in the industry.

Why? Because I wasn't requiring them to sit in a cubicle from eight to six *plus* be on call 24/7. On the contrary, I was offering part-time, work-from-home jobs that only required face time when something significant was happening at the port. I found people were lining up to work for me—even for fewer hours and less money—because of the greater life quality it afforded them.

And, beyond saving time and money, I was delivering a higher quality product. Over and over we would run into competitor shipping companies that were jealous of the quality of planning and management we were able to achieve. But why was our product so much better?

Because the analogous work at competitor companies had been outsourced overseas. I had started my business right around the time port workers in the US had begun unionizing, and in response, the industry began cutting jobs in the US and hiring workers on the other side of the globe. That meant our competitors' planning and management operations were being handled by people twelve time zones away, earning a fraction of the pay, and it translated to a less engaged and less skilled workforce. The upshot was costly mistakes.

That was how **I learned the difference between *cheap* and *efficient*.**

It was *cheap* for the other shipping companies to outsource jobs overseas. Their budgets looked great, since they'd cut labor costs by 50 percent or more. But it turned out that those cheaper workers actually cost more than they saved, in the form of mistakes and miscommunication.

Meanwhile, it was *efficient* for me to hire the best vessel planners in the business on a part-time basis, leverage their time and talents with the best technology available, and then train unskilled workers to handle related clerical work. It was so efficient, in fact, that over a ten-year contract with my client, **I reduced costs by nearly 50 percent and saved the company *millions* of dollars.**

I also now had a great team of staff at my own business, which was good because I decided I didn't want to devote my life to the shipping business after all.

Instead, I decided to go to law school.

A few years later, still managing the shipping company on a part-time basis, I emerged with my law degree. I thought I wanted to have my own legal practice, so I took the time to observe how other lawyers had set up practices and operated their firms.

And what I saw reminded me of the very thing I'd learned in international shipping.

Many of the lawyers I met had founded their own practice with the simple goals of developing expertise in their particular area of law, and serving their clients accordingly. Frequently they started practicing with nothing more than a home office. But soon they had to divide their time between legal practice on the one hand, and marketing and bookkeeping on the other. Then, once their practice had grown a bit and it was time to hire a legal secretary, that raised questions about how to attract qualified applicants, and what kind of salary to offer, not to mention renting office space. Then came all the issues of office management, from IT to payroll to fixing the copy machine to taking out the trash at the end of the day.

Soon it got so these lawyers were doing anything *but* the practice of law, because they were so busy running the day-to-day operations of the firm. Still worse, the fact that they were spending all their time on operations instead of law meant they were doing mediocre work for their clients. That made it difficult to attract new clients and thereby grow their practice. And they certainly didn't have the time to stay on top of changing legal theory, or to network and attend conferences. On top of all that, they were just basically unhappy since they were spending all their time doing stuff they weren't very good at and had never had any desire to do in the first place.

Just like in the shipping business, **time was undervalued, and thus mismanaged—and business was suffering as a result.**

The Start-up Capital You Didn't Know You Had

Business owners across industries undervalue their time for a very simple reason: They're not thinking about what they're giving up. For every hour they spend fighting with QuickBooks, and trying to fix their own website, and plowing through a mountain of paperwork, and doing everything *but* the business itself, there's a cost. The cost is what they could have done instead. Here's what I mean by that:

I'm guessing you have a wish list for your business. Maybe on that wish list there's an idea for a new product. Maybe there's an idea for how to make an existing product even better. Or maybe there's a plan for how to reach a whole new market. These sorts of ideas might come to you all the time; you're a creative person, after all, since entrepreneurs are creative by their very nature. But now that you're drowning in the daily humdrum tasks of just keeping your business afloat, your ideas get relegated to a wish list—or, more accurately, a when-I-finally-have-time list. And at the rate you're going, you can't imagine *ever* having time to get to those ideas, even though you know they have the potential to grow your business in new and exciting ways.

That's the cost of doing your own bookkeeping. That's the cost of managing HR and payroll on your own, and sitting on hold with the cable company when Internet service goes down. **For every hour you spend on those boring tasks, you're giving up an hour in which you could have made your business better. That's why it's *time*—not money—that ultimately drives your bottom line.**

Your business will be wildly successful to the extent you're using your time to become the very best in your niche, whether that niche is container shipping or practicing a specific type of law or serving pizzas in a small town. **To the extent that you're making your business the very best it can possibly be in its unique niche, you're carving out a powerful place in the world—but to the extent you're not, you're not.**

And that's why **transitioning your business from one that's bogged down in operations to one that's hyper-focused on the business itself means fundamentally changing the way you think about your time.** Every hour you spend on QuickBooks is an hour you didn't make your business greater, and that's a cost you can't afford. **The key is to transform the way you use your time, from DIYing to focusing on what you do best and how to do it even better.**

This might surprise you, but changing your mindset in this way requires putting a dollar value on your time. Why? Because that dollar value will act as a guide in helping you delegate the tasks that are inefficient for you to do yourself. In the next chapter we'll walk through the process of determining how much an hour of your time is worth. For now, though, we'll simply acknowledge that **your time has a dollar value—and it's probably higher than you think.**

To illustrate what I mean, think for a second about a Silicon Valley entrepreneur who's lucky enough to have someone invest in her start-up. Let's say the investor ponies up $5 million for the entrepreneur's idea. The entrepreneur then has to devise the smartest way to use that $5 million to build the business from scratch.

You might think that scenario is nothing like your own, since you're bootstrapping your business by patching together savings, running on a scant budget, and DIYing everything you can. But no business gets off the ground without start-up capital. It's just that in the case of the Silicon Valley entrepreneur, there was an outside investor, while you're self-funding. You don't have $5 million to dedicate to self-funding, of course, but you are using something else of value: your time.

Remember, you gave up your old salary in order to work for yourself. And every day that goes by in which you decide not to go back into the labor force—either part-time or full-time—you continue to double-down on that decision. Well, *the salary you're giving up is like that $5 million of investment capital.* Instead of using your time to earn wages from someone else, you're investing it into growing your business. And **just like an entrepreneur carefully spending down $5 million of start-up capital, you should be laser-focused on how you're using your time, because your time *is* your start-up capital.**

There are three key questions you should continually ask yourself. These questions will help you maintain that laser focus and thus make smart decisions with the precious twenty-four hours in each day:

1. **Where am I spending my time?**
2. **What is the cost of my labor?**
3. **How much value am I adding to my business?**

In the coming chapters we'll return to these questions again and again. We'll put a dollar figure on each hour of your work. We'll examine which tasks are—and aren't—worthy of your personal attention. We'll zero in on the value you add to your business by doing the things only you can do. And then we'll delegate the other stuff.

Think you can't afford to delegate? You can't afford *not* to.

In the pages ahead, we'll explore how delegating actually *saves* money, all while freeing up your most precious resource: your time. **From building a world-class team to understanding how passion *is* efficiency to breaking up the "value chain" in order to get the best work from a great staff while paying good wages *and* improving your bottom line, the pages ahead are packed with everything you need to know to make your business better, smarter, more profitable, and ready for a new phase of growth.**

2

The Efficiency of Passion and the Power of Focus

It's hard to do a really good job on anything you don't think about in the shower.

—Paul Graham (Cofounder, Y Combinator)

You're willing to do just about anything to make your business a success, which is why you're not afraid of handling yet another problem with your supplier, or taking the trash to the dumpster at the end of another long day, or staying up late on Friday night to finally balance the account books. You had the courage to start your own business, and with that courage, you brought a ton of elbow grease. You were ready to do whatever tedious work was necessary to make that business a success.

And you were 100 percent correct that starting and running a business requires every ounce of commitment and courage and elbow grease you can muster.

But—contrary to all the popular wisdom out there—**building a successful business *doesn't* mean spending your days doing tedious work you despise**. Roll up your sleeves, yes, and get to work creating the enterprise you've imagined. You'll spend late nights devising new strategies for growth, yes, and you'll wake up in the middle of the night thinking about better ways to reach your target customer. But doing tedious, boring work? Nope, that's not in your job description.

Here's why: because LeBron James doesn't mow his own lawn.

Yes, you read that right. LeBron James doesn't mow his own lawn. LeBron is among the best basketball players ever to step on the court, and he has multimillion-dollar endorsement contracts with the likes of Nike and Coca-Cola. He also has, in his native state of Ohio, a beautiful home and green lawn, which he purchased after his ascent to superstardom. That home and lawn are symbols of his success, and he wants that lawn to look perfect.

But he sure doesn't mow it himself.

There are plenty of reasons for that, and some are more obvious than others. For one, his time is better spent elsewhere: improving his free throw and filming endorsement commercials, for example. If you were to ask an economist why LeBron doesn't mow his own lawn, that economist will wax poetic about how it would be *irrational* since LeBron can earn lots of money doing other things in the same amount of time and then he can put a fraction of those earnings toward hiring a professional groundskeeper. But if you actually asked LeBron the reason, his answer might be a lot simpler:

"Because mowing my lawn is boring."

Boredom Economics

Did you know there are serious researchers who devote their careers to understanding how boredom affects productivity at work? And according to their research, there's a close relationship between boredom and inefficiency.[3]

To combat the problem, economists have come up with strategies that business owners can deploy to make their bored workforce more productive. One such strategy is to pay employees more. That's an expensive technique, but apparently, money has a way of making things less boring. Another strategy is to set goals and then measure and report progress, which can turn tasks into a sort of game.

But if you're a small-business owner with the freedom to design your own workforce, a far better solution is to make sure no one is doing tasks he or she considers boring. It's just too expensive.

One of the reasons LeBron is so great at the game of basketball is because he loves it. He's loved it since he was a kid; there's nothing that gets him more fired up than stepping out on the court and competing. Averaging nearly thirty points a game, he puts on a spectacular show for his fans. You can actually *see* his passion at work. Meanwhile, he thinks lawn mowing is boring.

And the fact that he finds it boring is actually an important emotional indicator. It's a signal telling him how to allocate his time—that he *shouldn't* use precious hours for lawn mowing. Meanwhile, his passion for basketball serves the same purpose: It's directing him back onto the court, where he excels.

And it's no surprise he excels, because when you're fanatical about something in the way LeBron is about basketball, you think about it all the time. You think about how to do it better. You think about ways it's never been done before. And you want to avoid or race through everything else on your schedule, just so you can get back to that thing you're passionate about. As Paul Graham, the cofounder of the Silicon Valley accelerator Y Combinator has noted, "It's hard to do a really good job on anything you don't think about in the shower." LeBron has that passion for basketball, and he listens to that powerful signal—and then he hires a lawn-care expert to handle the mowing.

You may not be a professional basketball player, but the same logic still applies to you. You're passionate about what you do; you wouldn't have started your own business if you weren't. You're an entrepreneur with a vision for turning your passion into a successful enterprise. Just as LeBron follows his passion, you're following yours. (And if you've lost that passion over the years, keep reading. This book is all about helping you find that passion once again, and then unleashing it!)

But how about those account books you haven't found the time to balance?

If you're like most entrepreneurs, you find accounting boring as hell. The same goes for HR paperwork and setting up IT systems. And *the fact that you find these things boring is an important signal.* It's a signal that spending your valuable time on those tasks is inefficient.

Because while passion engenders energy and innovation, boredom does the opposite. When you find something boring, you avoid thinking about it. You procrastinate, putting it off as long as you possibly can. Then when it finally comes time to do it, you muddle through and do work that's perhaps mediocre, if not worse. And that's only natural: You're unhappy doing it, so of course your output isn't great.

> "You'll find boredom where there is the absence of a good idea."
>
> —Earl Nightingale (American Writer, 1921–1989)

In other words, **boring equals inefficient. And when it comes to running a business, inefficient equals less competitive, and less competitive means you're on your way to obsolescence. That's why the success of your business depends on whether or not you're going to stop doing the boring stuff.** Like LeBron, you've got to find someone else to mow the lawn—or, in your case, balance the account books, or handle HR, or IT, or the many other things you've attempted to DIY.

Luckily, there are people in this world who are passionate about accounting. There are people in this world who are passionate about setting up great IT systems. There are even people in this world who are passionate about tax law (trust me on that one; I went to law school with a bunch of them). And all of these people will find better, faster, and more innovative ways of handling the seemingly boring parts of your business than you ever could. Meanwhile, there are people in this world who think whatever *you're* passionate about is a snooze fest. And **that's why you should focus on doing what you do best—and enjoy the privilege of getting paid to do it—while also bringing in specialists to handle the other stuff for you.**

Now it's time for the trillion-dollar question: **How can you possibly *afford* to hire the expertise you need so that you can focus your own time and attention on the core of your business?**

Here's how:

The Golden Formula

To illustrate this concept, we'll pull inspiration from a client of mine who owns a liquor store in Williamsburg, New York. This guy is super knowledgeable about spirits of every type and variety, and it's immensely clear to everyone that he has all the passion and expertise he needs to establish a great business in one of New York's trendiest neighborhoods.

But how's he been spending his time?

Well, he started out on the same route as just about every other entrepreneur out there: He was DIYing. He was using his daytime hours to struggle through all the paperwork and permitting that's required for starting a liquor business in New York. Then, until the earliest hours of the morning, he was trying to use Squarespace to build his own website. He said he didn't have the money to pay an expert to do those things for him.

So I started talking with him about the value of his time. I asked how much money he used to make before investing himself in his start-up.

Turns out, he was making great money at his day job. In fact, he was pulling in around $85,000 a year. We put that into hourly terms, and figured he'd been making about $50 an hour. What's more, he had similar opportunities available to him to work part-time at that same rate, though he'd turned them down because he didn't have time.

"How many hours have you spent trying to make this website yourself?" I asked him.

He didn't know exactly, but at a minimum, it was *dozens* of hours. At $50 an hour, that was equivalent to spending at least $1,200 on Web design—and yet he had very little to show for it.

Let's revisit those three key questions I introduced in the last chapter.

1. **Where am I spending my time?**

   In the case of the Williamsburg entrepreneur, he was spending his time doing amateur Web-design work.

2. **What is the cost of my labor?**

   Since every hour he was working on his website was an hour he wasn't spending at a side job, he was effectively paying $50 an hour (by giving up that money) to do amateur Web-design work himself.

3. **How much value am I adding to my business?**

   We estimated his DIY Web-design efforts were worth approximately $10 hourly.

What had previously seemed like a sensible course of action—doing the website himself to save money—now looked ludicrous, since an expert designer could have knocked out that simple website in a couple hours, and for a price tag well under the $1,200 in wages he'd forfeited in order to do it himself.

So how did we proceed?

We worked out a plan in which he would pick up some hours at his day job and then use his earnings to pay experts who could quickly and skillfully accomplish the tasks necessary for getting his business off the ground. Then, in the hours he devoted to his business, he could focus on the business itself, which meant curating a world-class selection of spirits and getting to know his target customer. So all of a sudden, he went from struggling to get everything done—and continually pushing his grand-opening date further into the future—to having the initial paperwork and Web design behind him, and planning a launch that would impress his customers with greater selection and quality than he'd initially thought possible.

> Focus on being productive instead of busy.
>
> —Tim Ferriss (American Writer)

This goes back to the difference between cheap and efficient: **It was *cheap* for him to do everything himself, but it was *efficient* for him to pay someone else to turn out better, quicker results, while redirecting his own efforts to his area of expertise.**

Putting a dollar value to his time was essential. It made clear where his time was poorly spent, as in using $1,200 worth of labor to patch together a website worth almost nothing. But even more than that, it helped him focus on the areas where his time was *best* spent. He started considering an all-important question:

How could he use his $50-an-hour time to add *at least* $50 of value to his business for every hour he worked?

The answer was to dedicate himself to building a top-notch inventory, so his store would be a smash hit with his Williamsburg clientele. **Instead of effectively reducing his hourly rate to $10 or less by DIYing, he focused his energy toward the areas where he could add a huge amount of value, and thereby *increase* his hourly rate—probably many times over.**

And just like that, he had started to think like a successful entrepreneur. The most prosperous business owners are obsessed with their hourly rate, and increasing it all the time. You should be too.

And by your hourly rate I *don't* mean your annual salary. Let's say you bring in $100,000 a year. Not bad, right? Well, it makes a big difference whether you earned that $100,000 in four thousand hours—eighty hours a week, or about $25 an hour—or in two thousand hours, or forty hours a week and $50 an hour, instead.

So let's say it took you four thousand hours last year to bring in $100,000 working at your own business. And let's say you spent half of all that time handling invoicing, inventory, and accounting. Now consider you could hire someone at $30,000 a year to do that same work. That cuts your take-home salary down to $70,000, and it's painful, because now you're trying to support your family with less money. But **besides giving yourself a 40 percent raise in your hourly rate, you literally freed up half your time. And now you can take that time and use it to grow your business.** (And that holds true even if you need to use some of your newly free time to pick up outside work, the way our friend in Williamsburg did, in order to supplement your income.)

Or maybe you're not ready to hire a full-time employee. That's fine; this same formula applies on a smaller scale.

First, though, **you've got to put a dollar value on each hour of your time.** For some people, like lawyers, it's easy, because they bill by the hour. In other cases, it makes sense to use the salary you were earning before becoming an entrepreneur; in that case, simply divide by the number of hours you work in order to calculate your hourly rate. Or you can use a website like salary.com or glassdoor.com to estimate what you *would* be earning if you weren't running your own business, or what you *could* be earning if you found a way to take on some part-time or freelance work.

Now let's say you've figured out that an hour of your time is worth $30. And maybe you've been spending about six hours a week on bookkeeping; that means those six hours cost you $180, because that's what you could earn working six hours at a side job.

Now consider that you can easily find someone to do bookkeeping for you at $15 an hour. By hiring a part-time employee at that rate, you've suddenly cut your weekly bookkeeping costs in half *and* freed up six hours of your valuable time every week, in perpetuity. Not to mention the fact that once this new employee gets the hang of it, he'll probably do it in fewer than six hours (saving you still more money) because it's his specialty, and, for the same reason, he's likely to do a better job than you ever did.

Maybe you'll choose to use your newfound six hours to do some of that $30 work in a side job, and take home the extra $90-plus per week as income. Or maybe you'll choose to invest your time back into growing your business. Or maybe you'll do a mix between the two. **Either way, you just saved a bunch of time *and* money, just by doing something you thought you couldn't afford. *That's* the Golden Formula.**

Want to dig deeper into how to apply The Golden Formula to your business? Download the free whitepaper at: GF.WeDoBoring.com

---

From Fine Spirits to Twenty Thousand Miles of Oceanic Trade Lanes

This same strategy applies to your business no matter whether you're selling spirits in Williamsburg or legal services in Indiana, or whether you're managing container shipping from the Western hemisphere to the East and back again. **Regardless of what industry you're in, the efficiency of passion—and a driving focus on the value of your time—promises enormous gains in time saved, better output, and, over the long run, a far more valuable and profitable business.**

Searching for What You Do Best

Ever wondered why Google's home page is just pure white space with a search field in the middle?

Back in 1999, when the Google team began to add additional content to the home page, they started receiving anonymous e-mails. Those e-mails contained just a single number: 37, then 43, and so on.[4] What was the significance of the number? Soon the team figured out that it was the number of words cluttering the formerly pristine home page.

More than fifteen years later, Google.com remains completely focused on the one thing that made the company famous: Web search.

It's precisely this logic that allowed me to improve efficiency in the seemingly oddball world of international shipping. International shipping and your typical entrepreneur actually have a lot in common: They're both trying to do a lot of things—too many things, in fact. While most entrepreneurs are busy DIYing every aspect of their business instead of specializing, shipping companies are *also* juggling a million different things. They charter ships. They have contracts with rail lines to help facilitate moving cargo from ports to places like Chicago. They coordinate with freight companies. And they manage all the marine operations of where their ships should go and how they should stow all the containers. All of these things are necessary parts of international shipping. But at the end of the day, what's the core work of a shipping company? What's its *single most important activity*, like basketball for LeBron?

It's connecting buyers on one side of an ocean to sellers on the other.

In order words, the shipping company's core business is to create trade lanes. A trade lane is like a bus route; it's a plan for a route across the ocean, and for what stops to include along the way. Every single day, shipping companies have to make complex, strategic decisions about the routes their ships will take, with millions of dollars riding on the outcome. That's the core of international shipping.

But **with so many different parts to their business, it's easy for executives at these companies to get distracted, the same way entrepreneurs divert their attention away from their passion and then use their time for DIY Web design and accounting or a host of other tasks.** Executives at shipping companies start to think that marine operations and stowage—that is, deciding how each container should be stowed and dealing with all the legal regulations and logistics—are their core business. That's a costly mistake.

All it took to turn that thinking on its head was for one shipping company to recognize the wisdom in outsourcing to a specialist. At my little start-up, we made marine operations the absolute core of our business; it became our unyielding passion. Then we brought on our first client. All of a sudden, that client was saving nearly 50 percent on its marine operations and enjoying a far higher quality of planning and management. We were outcompeting other shipping companies at their own game.

Even when it comes to moving cargo twenty thousand miles along oceanic trade lanes, running a smart, efficient business means identifying the core of what you do, and letting someone else do the rest. It means adopting the most powerful and time-tested business plan in the world: "Do less, better."

Do less, better.

The efficiency of passion means there just isn't room for mediocrity in the marketplace, because someone who's more passionate and more focused will swoop in and gobble up your market share. That's why **the sooner you become laser-focused on what you do best—and find specialists to build a team that will handle the other stuff—the sooner you'll outstrip the competition and see your business grow.**

Of course, that requires finding the right people. That's next.

3

The Big Idea: Flipping the Pyramid

None of us is as smart as all of us.

—Ken Blanchard (American Writer)

So far, this book has been pure celebration of all the benefits you'll reap from specializing in your area of expertise and delegating everything else. But I'm not saying it's *easy* to make that huge change to the way you run your business.

It absolutely *won't* be easy.

And one of the reasons it won't be easy is because it means trusting other people with the business you've built.

After all, you've put in a lot of hard work learning how to do everything yourself. You started out knowing nothing about accounting, and you developed your own chart of accounts that makes sense to you, and your own method in QuickBooks that makes sense to you, and your own system for invoicing and billing that makes sense to you. That system might not make a ton of sense to anyone else, but it's the way you've always done it, and to you, it's a Rembrandt.

And **maybe you *have* tried hiring other people. Maybe all they did was let you down.** Maybe you tried to teach someone your unique bookkeeping system, and that person didn't get it. So you thought, *Hell, I can do this myself faster than I can train him!* Then he made some mistakes—because new employees inevitably make mistakes. And after that, you fired him and went back to doing it yourself.

It's hard to trust other people with your business. The business is your baby, after all. You built it from the ground up with sheer force of will. You poured all your creative energy and time and pure muscle into it—so of course you don't want anyone screwing it up. Maybe watching someone else fumble around in your files or your accounting books or your inventory makes your shoulders seize up. You stand there picturing all the ways they could make a mess that *you'll* have to clean up. And then you lie awake at night, because you can't stop worrying about it.

And as if all of *that* weren't bad enough, **in the short term, bringing on new people is going to decrease your bottom line.** All of a sudden, you're paying good money to someone else for doing things you could have done yourself. That means you have less cash in your pocket and you're worrying about your business more than you ever did before.

By some estimates, 90 percent of all start-ups fail. Why?

It's generally estimated that between 80 and 90 percent of all start-ups fail.[5] Top reasons include a lack of product-market fit (that is, building a product that no one wants), failure to assemble a strong team, and ineffective allocation of resources, including money and time.[6]

I get it.

But even though it's uncomfortable to bring on help, and even though it will temporarily decrease your bottom line, it's the *only way* to turn your business into the success you know it can be.

For many small-business owners—like the solopreneur lawyer I described back in Chapter One—**the business has become nothing more than a treadmill.** You're working eighty hours a week, every week, year after year. Maybe you thought it would get easier after a few years, but it doesn't, and meanwhile, the business is just limping along. You're basically bringing in the same amount of money you did last year, and the year before, even as you keep working yourself to exhaustion.

That cycle will continue as long as you're bogged down in the minutiae of daily operations. And there's only one way to free yourself from that minutiae: Entrust it to others.

But I'm not suggesting that you simply hire whoever walks in the door. Just having warm bodies—at whatever wages, and at any quality of output—certainly isn't the answer.

Instead, **it's time to build the kind of high-quality, high-performance team that you thought only the biggest companies could afford.**

Flipping the Pyramid

A while back, a guy came to me after spending two years working tirelessly on his start-up. This guy wasn't your everyday entrepreneur; he'd gone to Harvard Law School, and he'd spent some time in a lucrative career at the consulting firm McKinsey & Company. Basically, he had more IQ points than he knew what to do with.

He also had a great idea for a business. During his time in law school, he saw there was a market for a networking site exclusive to law students. He envisioned a one-stop shop where students could connect and find all the expertise and notes and outlines and discussion forums they needed in order to excel. It was a unique vision, with a clearly defined market niche. That's powerful—not to mention that the guy himself was special; he had a really unique set of skills *plus* the entrepreneurial spirit.

Then he started coding.

By which I mean, he started DIYing the website. He got into the zeroes and the ones of code, and he was micromanaging an overseas team to try to get the site up and running on the cheap. He was in the HTML and the CSS and the JavaScript. He was wrestling with whether HostGator or GoDaddy or Site5 was a better place to host the site.

And believe me when I say, building websites was not his core competency. I have no doubt that, with all his brainpower, this guy was *capable* of learning how to write code and he was capable of micromanaging overseas developers with limited English proficiency. But he was starting from scratch; he had no knowledge in that area, never mind expertise. And it sure wasn't the reason he wanted to become an entrepreneur. It absolutely was *not* his passion. So, over the course of two years, he built a website that was, frankly, terrible.

I met him around that time, and we sat down to talk.

And though this guy had a really impressive resume and an idea with the potential to be worth tens of millions of dollars or more, we came to the conclusion that his stumbling block was the same one that nearly every entrepreneur faces: how to do the right things at the right time with the right resources. He was using all his time and energy to DIY the website, but now he couldn't get any further. He had done as much DIYing as he could do, and he was unhappy with the results.

When we talked it through, we concluded that the only road to success involved hiring a US-based staff with technical expertise to build the website he'd envisioned, or maybe even a better one. But there was one big problem: The standard price tag for that investment far exceeded his available budget for this project.

This is where the Golden Formula changed everything.

I asked about his work history, and eventually it came out that he was capable of commanding *$400 an hour* as an attorney or a consultant. Wow!

Would he be willing to pick up some outside work and use his earnings toward hiring experts to help him build the business, *better?*

"Sure," he said.

And suddenly, with that simple decision—and some creative partnerships we created in order to pay some people in equity or future royalties instead of cash—we had the freedom to begin designing the dream team he needed in order to build and launch his business. In other words, we were going to *flip the pyramid.*

To visualize what it means to flip the pyramid, think for a second about the typical management structure of a Fortune 500 company. There's a CEO sitting at the top; just below, there's a small team of executive management. Below them, there's middle management. And so on, all the way to the base of the pyramid, where there are perhaps thousands of employees handling the company's frontline operations.

Most entrepreneurs picture themselves building that typical management structure, with themselves at the top as CEO. Except, on the shoestring budget of a normal start-up, there's no money to build those layers of management below. So the entrepreneur finds himself with an upside-down pyramid. Instead of sitting at the top, the CEO is at the very bottom, beneath the dozens of different hats he's wearing as he DIYs the entire business. Beneath the weight of that upside-down pyramid, the CEO gets crushed under crippling weight, and thinks his only hope is to grow the business over time so that he can eventually start taking those hats off, one by one, and putting them on other people. Until that happens, though, the CEO is the Hat Juggler in Chief.

The upside-down pyramid

The vast majority of start-ups fail, and one of the biggest reasons is an inefficient and unsustainable management structure like that upside-down pyramid. Meanwhile, the roughly 10 percent of start-ups that survive do so because they've built a winning team.

What does a winning team look like?

It looks like a flipped pyramid.

Instead of remaining a lone CEO crushed under the weight of all the different jobs you're trying to perform, imagine turning that pyramid right side up, so that your business now has a team of experts whom you're managing from the top. *That's* your formula for success.

The flipped pyramid!

In the case of the website for law students, we got to work assembling the necessary team. We brought in the technical expertise required to build an elegant and user-friendly site that would be a hit with law students. We also brought on team members who'd been working on adjacent business models. There were people running sites that sold outlines for law classes, and people doing podcasts about some core topics in the law curriculum, and people blogging on related subject matter, and someone offering an online tutorial about how to excel at law-school exams. By creating partnerships with all of these adjacent businesses, we were able to bring in a ton of top-notch content on a very limited budget. With this approach, **the Web developers estimated we'd saved $750,000 in start-up costs and delivered a return on the founder's initial investment in excess of 3,500 percent.** Talk about increasing his hourly rate!

And that's why **one of your most important tasks as an entrepreneur is to build a strong team.** That doesn't necessarily mean you're going to hire a dozen staff members right away (although you might be doing that sooner than you think). Even if your team is just you and one part-time employee, or you and a Web designer who works three hours a month, or you and a legal secretary who only works on Tuesdays, **your job is to assemble a team that lifts you up and raises the value of each hour of whatever *you're* doing.**

From Concept to C-suite

This whole idea of "flipping the pyramid" might have worked for some guy who went to Harvard Law and had some money to spend, but how does it apply to your small business?

Think back to Chapter One, and the way the classic solopreneur lawyer starts and runs his own firm. Remember that lawyers tend to start out with a vision simply to practice law, but soon they're crushed under the weight of all the responsibilities of a small-business owner.

Now consider the opposite approach. What if that lawyer brought on a partner with deep experience in small-business operations management *before* he got himself into that mess? Let's say he brought in someone to act as his chief operations officer, his COO, to help build the firm.

How would the expertise of a COO improve the situation?

Well, I'd like to introduce you to Jim, a hypothetical solo attorney and small-business owner who decided to hire a COO to help him build a better business.

Right off the bat, Jim's COO suggested that his tiny law firm is probably a good candidate for a virtual office. So instead of committing to a two-year lease for a brick-and-mortar office space, he rented space designed specifically for virtual offices—space that gave him a very professional look for depositions and in-person meetings with clients, but that doesn't cost him rent for 365 days a year. Instead, he pays only for what he uses.

Then, to keep his files organized, the COO suggested going paperless, deploying a cloud-based document-management system to power his new firm. Jim *also* got a cloud-based PBX system with a virtual receptionist to answer the phone for him during business hours, so his busy schedule would no longer scare away potential clients.

Just by making those changes, Jim had already improved his bottom line by 15 percent. He's also made a strong start at building the team he needs at the top of the pyramid. His outsourced COO costs less than $1,000 a month, and pays for herself many times over. Furthermore, instead of DIYing all the IT and office management, Jim has expert service providers doing those tasks for him. In other words, **this solo lawyer has hired a ton of help and it's *saving* him money.**

And because of all that money he's saved just by running a more efficient infrastructure, he now has some extra cash to play with. His COO is helping him figure out how to bring in some new talent. But maybe he doesn't need full-time employees just yet. Of course, he *could* hire a $70,000-a-year paralegal, but actually, he only needs about ten hours a week of real paralegal work. He also needs approximately fifteen hours of legal secretarial work per week, which is more like $40,000-a-year work. And let's say he needs ten hours of transcription work, which pays around minimum wage. Now that lawyer sees he doesn't have to spend $70,000 for those services bundled together in a single employee.

So **instead of making a full-time hire, his COO encourages him to "break up the value chain."** That means all those different responsibilities can be separated and handled by different part-time help, and then compensated accordingly. So now there's one talented person who does part-time paralegal work, and another who does secretarial work. The transcription work goes to someone earning minimum wage.

Life Is Not a Zero-Sum Game

We'll dig deeper into the details of "breaking up the value chain" in Chapter Eleven. But for now, try to take on faith that when you create efficiency, you create wealth. You uncover ways to pick more metaphorical apples from the metaphorical tree. And when there are more apples to go around, it's better for everyone.

Creating wealth should create jobs, not eliminate them. If you have a great employee earning $70,000 a year, but he's spending part of his time on low-cost work like transcription or inventory, this same logic applies. Give that low-cost work to someone working part-time at minimum wage—and thereby create a job—and then reallocate your high-value employee's time so he's writing excellent blog content for your website, or doing something else that uses his best and highest talent to add corresponding value to your business.

Now, on top of the 15 percent this lawyer saved by running more efficient infrastructure, he's *also* just saved a fortune on labor costs. He's better off yet again.

With the savings starting to pile up, he's beginning to think about hiring a chief financial officer (CFO). We're not talking about someone who just does taxes, because everyone's got that. We're talking about an outsourced CFO who's going to do the bookkeeping, who'll give him quarterly reports, who'll do cash flow analysis, and who'll teach him about "Key Performance Indicators," also known as KPIs. Those KPIs will establish and track this particular law firm's definition of success. Plus, instead of fighting with QuickBooks until the darkest hours of the night, Jim has someone who's transformed QuickBooks into a powerful analytics tool. Suddenly, that program is giving him actionable insights about how to run his law firm better.

With the help of his COO and CFO, he's now making shrewd decisions that squeeze more profit out of the revenue he already has.

And we haven't even started talking about attracting new clients.

With everything going so well, Jim starts to focus on getting his name out there. He realizes that's hard to do; it actually takes a lot of time and effort to bring traffic to his website and thereby draw new clients. But now he can afford to hire a marketing strategist. And that strategist helps him laser-focus on exactly who his target clients are. Are they predominantly male or female? What age? What industry? And how can he demonstrate that he's providing *exactly the service* they want and need?

So Jim gets that customer archetype down to a science, and together with the strategist and his talented paralegal, the team starts to create high-quality Web content designed just for that customer. *Plus,* they bring on a part-time expert who lives in the world of search engine optimization; literally *all* this person does is study Google's algorithms to understand the best way to build a local Web presence.

And now all of a sudden, Jim's client base is growing by 20 percent a year, and he's making 20 percent more profit from every revenue dollar than he otherwise would—not to mention that he's finally having fun. After all, he never *wanted* to be a jack-of-all-trades who practices law only in the corners of his day. All he wanted was to be a lawyer at his own firm and to deliver great legal counsel to his clients, and now he's doing just that, because he's built a suite of experts around him. He's doing what he's passionate about. *That* is why he started a law firm.

And that's the power of bringing on experts who will help you run your business with the same level of efficiency and excellence as a firm that has a thousand employees—except without the costly overhead. That's what it means to flip the pyramid.

Bringing the C-suite to Main Street

So now you know that it's fruitless to spend your time building a million-dollar calculator, and that the efficiency of passion means LeBron should never mow his own lawn, and that your path to entrepreneurial success lies in raising the value of each hour of your time and then building an expert team around you.

Now it's time to get a little more specific. What will *your* small business C-suite look like?

4

The Small-Business C-suite: Five Experts Even the Smallest of Businesses Can't Live Without

Talent wins games, but teamwork and intelligence win championships.

—Michael Jordan (Basketball Legend)

Now you know that the vast majority of start-ups collapse within their first couple of years, and that one of the most common reasons is a failure to assemble a strong team. **This chapter is your teambuilding how-to guide. It will teach you how to put your business among the elite ranks of start-ups that don't just succeed, but also flourish.**

From the last chapter you know entrepreneurs regularly make the mistake of trying to operate with a management structure that looks like an upside-down pyramid, with the CEO crushed beneath the weight of the dozens of jobs she's trying to DIY. The solution is to flip the pyramid, and to build a small-business C-suite around you as CEO, so your business has both the know-how and the bandwidth to flourish.

Once completed, **the C-suite has five team members in addition to the CEO: the chief operating officer (COO), the chief legal officer (CLO), the chief financial officer (CFO), the chief human resources officer (CHRO), and, finally, the chief marketing officer (CMO).** Generally, the team is assembled in precisely this order for reasons that will start to come into focus in this chapter and which will become even clearer in the next section of this book.

Of course, your small business can't support full-time or even part-time salaries for these five positions. When you're first starting out, few—if any—of these are in-house positions. Remember the story of the law firm in the last chapter, and the potential to bring in a part-time, outsourced COO at a modest cost. In the case of Jim and his law firm, this new COO more than paid for herself by creating a smart and efficient operations plan. Then, with savings in his pocket, Jim brought in an outsourced CFO (he didn't need to hire a CLO, since he is a lawyer), who used the firm's financials to develop key insights about how to squeeze more profit from every revenue dollar. Soon, Jim was ready to add *another* team member, and then another.

In other words, the process of building your C-suite draws on a virtuous cycle: Each addition to the team—whether in-house or outsourced—makes valuable contributions to your business and, with time, creates room in the budget for your *next* team member. It goes back to **one of your most essential responsibilities as CEO: to assemble a team in which each individual member raises the value of your core business in excess of his salary.**

So, let's take a look at what a successful C-suite looks like.

Chief Operating Officer (COO)

As the founder and CEO of your own small business, you started out as an expert in your field. If you've got a pizza shop, your expertise is pizza. If you're a lawyer, you're an expert in your area of law. That expertise is what led you to start a business in the first place. But that doesn't necessarily mean you knew much about running and growing a business.

So now imagine you have both. You have all the power of your technical expertise, and your unique vision for the future of your company, *coupled with* the business acumen of having lived and breathed small-business operations across a range of industries for years.

Sounds powerful, doesn't it? And that's precisely what it's like to have an expert outsourced COO in your corner.

The COO's job description is difficult to define precisely, because it changes from company to company and depends on the

CEO to whom the COO reports. But, broadly speaking, **a COO's role is a mix of strategy and execution, with the overarching purpose of keeping "the business end" of the business running smoothly while assisting the CEO in refining and realizing her vision.**

An Investment That Pays for Itself

Regardless of your COO's specific mix of responsibilities, he should more than pay for himself. The good ones do, many times over. One study estimated that outsourcing business process operations—as to an expert outsourced COO—can reduce relevant costs by as much as 41 percent.[7]

A good COO will also help you prevent costly mistakes. Consider one area in which businesses frequently make expensive errors: hiring new employees. One study estimated that a bad hire can result in a ROI of around negative 300 percent.[8] *Your COO helps keep that devastating cost from ever hitting your balance sheet.*

The **strategy** dimension of the COO's job lies in working with the CEO to draft an operational road map. Part II of this book will explore this process in detail; for now, let's just say that this road map spells out how the business is going to grow from where it stands today—when it's perhaps nothing more than an idea—to the point where it will deliver a valuable product to its first customer, to growing a strong customer base and becoming the thriving enterprise the CEO envisions, and everything in between.

This kind of operations strategy is a critical and complex part of making any business work, and getting it right is a very specialized skill. There's a reason the largest and most successful companies in the world regularly spend millions of dollars hiring consulting firms: because even big companies with tons of internal expertise need help seeing the best way forward. Sometimes internal staff members are too close to the company to see the forest for the trees. In the same way a therapist can help patients discover new things about themselves, consultants often help companies discover new things. Plus, operations experts typically have worked with many companies across a range of industries, and have developed perspective and insight that would be impossible to achieve internally at a single organization. That's the kind of expertise you bring on with an expert outsourced COO.

Then there's the **execution** part of the COO's job, which looks very different from the strategy component. Execution is exactly what it sounds like: It's putting the plan into action. That means devising a workflow and then delegating the multitude of tasks that need to get done, from the one-time slog of building the company's infrastructure to the repetitive tasks of executing the business model on a daily basis.

How much should your COO focus on strategy versus execution? The answer is: It depends.

We assist a lot of small-business owners at Agents of Efficiency, which is the company I founded with the express purpose of helping small businesses do better business than ever before. AOE actually serves as an outsourced COO for small businesses in a wide variety of industries. So, what have we learned from that work about the COO's role?

We've learned that most small businesses need the COO to maintain a different mix of responsibilities at different times. When the business has barely gotten off the ground, there's not a whole lot of execution that needs to be done; at that stage, it's mostly strategy and planning. In other words, your typical solopreneur doesn't need a ton of help with execution because the enterprise is too small; there's just not much to execute. But he could really use an expert advisor to help him think through strategy. Then, over time, the COO's job needs to evolve to focus increasingly on execution. That's because the larger the business gets, the more moving parts there are, and the more people the COO must manage in order to execute the business model.

While the COO's job description depends in part on timing and on the company itself, as well as the CEO, some things remain constant. **It's critical that the COO is a seasoned professional who acts as the CEO's key advisor in business operations, because the CEO's expertise is in the business itself, and *not* in operations.** Remember, LeBron should be playing basketball and working with a coach to help him excel, while letting someone else mow the lawn. Similarly, the CEO should be focused on the core business, and the COO should be pulling the strings behind the scenes.

And one of the key behind-the-scenes responsibilities your COO will handle—and the reason you hired a COO before anyone else—is figuring out how to build the rest of your C-suite. And the next member of the C-suite is essential, yet often unappreciated: the CLO.

Chief Legal Officer (CLO)

When we ask small-business owners around the country about their biggest complaints, one of the most common has to do with regulations and red tape. In fact, according to *The Economist*, **22 percent of small businesses say that red tape is their biggest problem.**[9] What many small-business owners fail to appreciate, however, is that this is a headache that all but goes away if you have a good CLO in your corner—especially if that CLO is working in concert with a good CFO and CHRO. And that's just one of the benefits of having a good CLO in your small-business C-suite.

Most people think of lawyers the way they think of heart surgeons: You eat Big Macs for years and don't exercise, and after a couple decades and a heart attack, you find a good surgeon. In other words, you only get a lawyer when things are really, *really* bad.

In fact, a lawyer should act more like a primary-care physician: someone who helps you develop a healthy lifestyle and keeps you in good shape, so you never need to see a heart surgeon—or, in this case, a litigator. In this way, lawyers actually save you both time and money.

That's why retaining legal counsel should be your first priority after your COO has helped you establish your start-up strategy. Skipping this step is the ultimate way of confusing *cheap* with *efficient*. Sure, it's *cheap* to spend twenty hours scouring the Internet in order to understand the relevant regulations for your industry, and another twenty hours figuring out how to draft ownership agreements between you and your founding partners, and another twenty on contract terms related to your vendor agreements, and for your employee contracts, and so on. These legal complexities are probably the most bewildering terrain a small-business owner has to navigate, and the most reckless to DIY.

In all those hours of late-night legal research on the Web—in which you used your scarce, high-value time—you likely *still* haven't fully understood the relevant legalese, and you're very likely making one, or two, or many, costly mistakes in all of your contracts and vendor relationships and corporate structure and permitting.

Meanwhile, **for each legal question that arises, a fifteen-minute call with your outsourced CLO could probably get you the answers you need**. Your CLO is someone who lives, breathes, and sleeps this stuff. So he can hand you answers on a silver platter, and thereby prevent future lawsuits, penalties, and a range of ugly costs that you never budgeted for and can't afford.

> Ninety percent of everything I dealt with as an attorney could have been avoided with a couple hours of up-front legal counsel long before a lawsuit ever developed.

You might think that's overly cautious, and that it's very unlikely that you'll ever get sued. Not so—and I know this all too well. I spent part of my career as an attorney in New York City, and **90 percent of everything I dealt with as an attorney could have been avoided with a couple hours of up-front legal counsel *before* a lawsuit ever developed.**

Because, regardless of what industry you're in, your business ultimately trades in relationships. And relationships can be messy, and sometimes end badly, with a devastating effect on your bottom line. Conversely, well-managed relationships help turn your business into a well-oiled machine. **No successful corporation would ever consider operating without a general counsel as an essential part of its C-suite, and neither should you.**

Here are just seven of the many possible ways your expert outsourced CLO can save you (tons of) money:

Corporate Structure

The decision about how to incorporate your business is a major one, and it has enormous tax and legal consequences down the road. It's also important to get this right on your first try, because it's very difficult—and often costly—to change your designation down the road. A CLO will match your small business with the appropriate corporate structure, whether it be an S Corp, an LLC, a Partnership, and so on.

I've encountered plenty of small-business owners who did some DIY research and hurriedly incorporated as an S Corp, then failed to hold annual meetings of their board of directors or shareholders, and commingled business and personal funds. With those missteps, they left themselves open to what's called "piercing the corporate veil." That is, they're vulnerable to lawsuits. Anyone can point at their business and say, "This whole corporation is a sham. It's really just Bob with a fancy name." When that happens, the legal protection you thought you had disappears. **A CLO keeps a watch on corporate activity to make sure operations are within the relevant legal boundaries.**

What's more, many entrepreneurs wrongly believe their S Corp or LLC status makes them lawsuit-proof. Not so. If you behave with negligence, *you* will get sued— personally. Period. Your corporate structure will protect you if an employee is negligent, or if there's a breach of a contract that has financial implications specific to the business itself, or something else that wasn't due to negligence on your part. But **if you're negligent, *you*—in addition to your company—will get sued. A CLO can help protect you from that risk.**

Tax Efficiency

People often think of accountants when they think taxes, but in terms of tax *strategy*, a good tax lawyer usually has a broader understanding of the tax code than a CPA. That's why all the biggest accounting firms in the nation are stacked with attorneys from the best law schools—because the tax code is fundamentally a set of laws. **A good CLO will navigate those laws on your behalf, and come up with a strategy to make your business as tax efficient as possible.**

Of course, you want a good CLO who's working hand-in-hand with a good CFO on your tax planning. That's why we're building a five-part C-suite; while each expert adds value in his or her own right, he or she adds the greatest value as a team. Your CLO and CFO work together to guarantee you're not paying more in taxes than you need to.

Regulatory Compliance

Don't mess with Uncle Sam. This is yet another situation in which it's infinitely smarter to get it right the first time than trying to correct missteps down the road. This is obviously essential to restaurants and bars; I've seen many get shut down because they were out of compliance, then never reopen.

But there are federal and state regulations governing your business regardless of your industry. For instance, the US has labyrinthine labor laws. Meanwhile, President Obama made the pursuit of employee misclassification an explicit priority for his administration, and that trend has yet to reverse. Yet a lot of small business owners play fast and loose around compensating workers as independent contractors or employees. On top of that, there are also overtime regulations, minimum-wage laws, and a whole lot of other complexity you don't have the time to deal with yourself.

Complying with the relevant regulations is crucial to operating a successful business, and your CLO keeps you on the right side of the law. Otherwise, you're playing Russian roulette.

Partner Relationship Management

It's pleasant to imagine that your relationship with your founding partners will always be amicable, and that as you build the business and, hopefully, draw profit from it, you'll always see eye-to-eye. But if things don't turn out that way—as they don't for so many—then a lack of good contracts will cost you dearly.

The vast majority of partnerships are founded with very little thought or planning. Oftentimes there's a fifty-fifty split simply because there are two partners, or 33.3 percent each for three partners, even when everyone isn't making equal contributions. That will bite you down the road when the business becomes successful. In fact, since the vast majority of start-ups fail, most poorly structured partnerships never come to light. But for those that succeed, founders' equity is a near universal problem.

Of course, dividing equity is complicated. Actually, it's really, really complicated. One person works many more hours to get the business off the ground; how does that affect her ownership stake? Another person came up with the idea; what's that worth? Another person gave up a lucrative career; does that matter?

A smart CLO can help. The right approach is to devise what are called "dynamic equity splits," in order to account for the many variables and to create the fairest—and most transparent—division of ownership. **The CLO helps to minimize the chances of a divorce between you and your cofounders, and provide the least painful path if a divorce does happen.**

Your CLO will also help you plan for a scenario even worse than strife among founders: failure. As much as you'd rather not think about it, failure is always an option in the cold, cruel world of start-ups. A CLO helps you figure out what failure looks like; at what point are you putting good money after bad? What's the key decision point at which you realize you'd be better off doing something else? I know: You don't want to think about it, which is why you've got a great lawyer.

Employee Relationship Management

Most small businesses lack the infrastructure to hire and retain employees in a way that minimizes legal risk. The risks are large and small, and come from more directions than most entrepreneurs readily appreciate.

A CLO will make sure you set clear expectations with employees from the outset: clear job descriptions, good contracts, and a thorough employee handbook. Because **when the expectations aren't clearly set, there are inevitable gaps between the employer's and the employees' expectations. That's when an expensive mess ensues. Happily, it's easily avoided with a CLO.** Trust me: Discrimination and wrongful-termination suits are a hell you can't afford.

Vendor Relationship Management

When it comes to vendors, having your own lawyer is crucial—in part, just because the *other* guy has a lawyer. That means, **before**

you even get to the negotiating table, your counterparts have written a bunch of legalese to stack the odds in their favor.

Having a CLO on your side means you don't have to acquiesce to whatever unfair terms your vendor sets out. Instead, you can neutralize their advantage, and then negotiate for a better deal. This is a yet another way a good CLO pays for himself.

Customer Relationship Management

Ever thought about why you have to agree to hundreds of pages of "terms and conditions" in order to use an Apple product? It might not be the best strategy, but that's the company's way of setting expectations with its consumers.

You probably want to steer away from dense legal agreements with your own customers, but **you *do* want to make sure that you and your customers are on the same page from day one. Your goal is to stay out of court. And your CLO works hard so you never see the inside of a courtroom.**

Chief Financial Officer (CFO)

It's all about the numbers. Your business is successful to the extent it's profitable. That's why, as soon as money starts coming in, the next member of your small-business C-suite should be your CFO. This is someone dedicated to squeezing as much profit from each revenue dollar as possible, while also reducing expenses.

But that's complicated. **Most of us don't have the expertise, or time, to read financial documents and then translate them into key insights and actionable strategy. That's why you've got your expert outsourced CFO: She's the one who makes sense of it all.**

Everyone's got an accountant for tax season. And that's useful, because certainly you shouldn't be doing your own taxes. But that's not what we're talking about here. We're talking about something much bigger. Your CFO evaluates your company's financial documents, provides essential information to your COO, and, in turn, your COO uses that information to help you make smarter choices about the company's operational strategy. **The CFO thereby converts your accounting books from a repository of receipts into an analytical tool. All of a sudden, your financials become a powerful resource in making sense of your business operations, including evaluating operational and marketing strategies implemented by your COO and your CMO** (we'll get to the CMO in a minute).

Just as the CLO's job is to consider what failure looks like, it's the CFO's job to determine what success looks like. To that end, she comes up with the Key Performance Indicators (KPIs) your company should obsess about, and ways to measure those KPIs so you can continually improve internal performance. **What are the baby steps that your company will take this month, and this quarter, and next quarter, to improve? What are you doing well and what are you doing poorly in each area? What goals do you want to set?**

On a more basic level, your CFO can also handle delegation of accounting operations, so that you, the CEO, never again have to think about that side of the business. Research by Deloitte Consulting found that handing off various billing processes to outside experts saved companies up to 55 percent on those costs. Your CFO will help you realize those savings and thereby improve your bottom line.[10]

Your CFO also works with your CLO to formulate the most efficient and forward-thinking tax strategy that's attainable for your company. That means coming up with a strategy in advance; by the time it's March of 2017 and an accountant is preparing your taxes, there's no opportunity for strategy. At that point, it's just about filling in the boxes.

Instead, I'm talking about developing a tax strategy before the year even begins. That's when an expert CFO who specializes in this stuff can work with your CLO to produce a tactical plan—a plan to see a significant ROI through smart cash-flow management. That means accounting for the time value of money. It means putting your capital to work for you to maximize interest. And it means minimizing taxes.

Every big company out there spends a lot of time on these complex financial questions in order to capture every last penny. But almost no small company does. Your CFO will make you one of the few, and give you the advantage you need to compete and succeed.

How to Manage Your Business like Google

Ever wonder how two kids named Larry Page and Sergey Brin managed to grow an idea and a laptop into a company valued at nearly half a trillion dollars?

While their story is complex, one simple answer is that they are a data-driven company. They make smart decisions about how to move forward based on data, not merely intuition and instinct. And companies like Google, LinkedIn, and Intel unite their teams behind data-driven goals through a management methodology known as OKRs, short for "objectives and key results."

> *While getting into the details of this management technique is beyond the scope of this book, the short story is that everything revolves around getting the team united behind short-term goals that are designed to move the needle on one (or maybe a couple) key metrics in a given month or quarter. Everyone knows what the goals are, their own role in getting there, and how they'll measure success.*
>
> *This type of clarity and focus is within your grasp if you're armed with the right tools and a good CFO.*

Chief Human Resources Officer (CHRO)

When a small-business owner brings in Agents of Efficiency to provide strategy and execution for its business's operations, the first question we ask is, "What's boring to you? Define boring."

And what do we hear most often?

Payroll.

Benefits.

Employee management and regulations.

Because of the efficiency of passion, LeBron should never mow his own lawn, and you should never do the boring HR stuff you hate.

That's one of the reasons why the next addition to your C-suite—just as soon as you hire your first employee—should be an outsourced CHRO.

The other reason is because he's going to save you money.

Most small-business owners have never heard of Professional Employer Organizations (PEOs). A PEO is a company that provides outsourced employee management. Not only does a PEO handle payroll, benefits, workers' compensation, and other relevant functions, it actually becomes the employer of record for the IRS. That means the only employee-related responsibility you maintain is managing job performance; that is, you stay focused on the core business and let someone else handle the boring (but essential) administration.

But wait, it gets better.

When you go this route, you save big. *Huge*. According to polling data, companies that outsource payroll and HR save *20 percent* on those costs. Then you save yet again on fines and penalties, because a whopping 33 percent of small businesses incur some sort of fine every year for making a payroll mistake, and that goes away as soon as you bring in a PEO.

But here's the big one: **The companies that outsource HR on average grow about 9 percent faster than other small businesses.**[11] Do you want to grow 9 percent faster than your competitors? Of course you do! So stop wasting internal resources on HR management when there are experts out there ready to do it for you.

It makes sense, of course, that there are such great savings to be had by making this relatively small change. **When you get sucked into the black hole of labor laws and health-care regulations and the bimonthly payroll treadmill, you're adding zero value to your business.**

Expunging those tasks from your universe saves huge amounts of time. For businesses with one to nine employees, outsourcing HR translated into time savings of seven hours per week.[12] You can redirect those hours toward making your business better.

Seven hours per week. Faster growth to the tune of 9 percent. Your CHRO pays for itself, many times over.

Chief Marketing Officer (CMO)

Before your business is ready for rapid growth, you have to be sure you have the right infrastructure in place to absorb all the new customers; otherwise, you'll suffocate under the weight of your success. That might sound like a good problem to have, but if, all of a sudden, you have a wave of new customers whom you can't serve, you'll quickly develop a bad reputation.

That's why the Chief Marketing Officer is the last member of your C-suite. Under your leadership, your COO, CLO, CFO, and CHRO build out the necessary infrastructure so your business is ready for a new phase of growth. Then it's time to bring on your CMO. And you *do* need a CMO.

I talk to small-business owners all the time who are proud that they don't have a marketing strategy. "We've never spent a dime on marketing, and we're doing just fine," they tell me. Meanwhile, they spend countless (and uncounted) hours on networking events, blogging, and all sorts of marketing activities. But they're not keeping track of those activities, so they don't show up in the account books.

More often than not, this non-strategy approach ends up being the most expensive marketing strategy you can have. After properly valuing the time it takes to engage in all those activities, the ROI on those marketing efforts frequently ends up being *negative*.

A CMO can turn that around.

In fact, the CMO's role is more straightforward than any of those we've just talked about: His job is to bring in new customers. It's that simple. If you have a CMO who's not more than paying for himself with new revenue, then fire him. (This is another reason you've got to have your expert COO and CFO in place well before you bring on a CMO: because your CFO is the one who can tell you how well—or poorly—your marketing efforts are performing. Then your COO can help you use those insights to adjust your strategy going forward.)

When your company first starts marketing, you won't know which tactics are the wisest to pursue. E-mail? Facebook? Blogging? Digital advertising? Print? Billboards? TV? Radio? Handing out flyers on the street? Networking? A great storefront? What's the strategy that will deliver the biggest ROI for every dollar you invest?

If that sounds like a complicated question, it is. And that's why you've got an expert strategist to help you think it through. When you're first starting out, your company has very limited bandwidth; you just don't have the resources to try all those different strategies at once. Your CMO helps you make smart choices to get your initial campaigns off the ground, all the while working with your COO to ensure these efforts are part of a cohesive business model and branding strategy. Then he works with your CFO to evaluate the effectiveness of those efforts and to continually improve. Eventually, your efforts become increasingly targeted and efficient—but that takes a little while.

What's essential is that you have an expert at the helm of this process. Because anyone can start blogging. Anyone can set up Google AdWords. Anyone can have a Facebook account. But using those tools to actually bring in more customers and increase profitability? That's an art form.

Google AdWords alone is immeasurably complex. Your CMO will enlist someone who lives in those algorithms, and who takes just a few minutes to set up smart campaigns for your company. The same goes for search engine optimization: It's the sort of thing that's laughable to DIY, since there are people who dedicate their entire careers to it. You can't compete with that. Don't try.

Meanwhile, there are zillions of small-business owners who blog. Why do they blog? Usually because someone told them they should. But do they have a strategy behind it? Do they know how much it costs to use their time for blogging, relative to how much new profit it brings in? (Remember, it all goes back to our three key questions from Chapter One: Where am I spending my time? What is the cost of my labor? How much value am I adding to my business?) Most small-business owners don't know the answers to those questions, but *you* will.

This is where your CMO, COO, and CFO join forces. The COO helps you define your broader business-model strategy. The CMO works within that plan to dial in the marketing strategy, and then executes it. The CFO provides important insights, like your Customer Acquisition Cost (CAC) and the Lifetime Value (LTV) of a customer, in order to evaluate success (you'll read more about your CAC and LTV in Chapter Fifteen). It's a process that ushers in the kind of growth you always knew your business could achieve. As just one example, one estimate of e-mail marketing found that its average ROI was an astonishing 38:1—that is, it returned $38 for every $1 spent. And one in five companies reported a ROI greater than 70:1![13]

What's clear is the immense value of bringing on an expert to navigate the complicated—and lucrative—world of marketing on your behalf. What's at stake? Merely the growth, and future, of your company.

The Reimagined Role of the CEO

Now we've flipped the pyramid and built an expert team around you, the CEO, in order to focus, streamline, evaluate, protect, and expand the value of your core business. With all of these team members handling their area of expertise and joining forces to make your business bigger and better than it's ever been, what's left for *you* to do? Plenty. That's next.

PART II

A NEW ROAD MAP FOR EFFECTIVE SMALL-BUSINESS OPERATIONS

Did you write a business plan once upon a time, but haven't looked at it in years? If so, toss that useless sucker in the trash. Or do you not even *have* a business plan, and feel guilty about it? If so, feel guilty no more.

For most small businesses, a formal business plan is practically worthless. But that doesn't mean you shouldn't have a plan. In this section of the book, you'll discover a much simpler and more powerful tool for mapping your road to success. Then you'll follow an entrepreneur by the name of Sue, and her newly founded bagel business, through what's called the Efficiency Roadmap process: the journey from drowning in your small business to thriving in it.

In this section, you'll find:

1. Why the product or service you sell is *not* the core of what you do and what your business's core *really* is.
2. The planning tool your business actually needs (I promise it's not a business plan), and how to use that tool to chart a powerful path to growth.
3. The key elements of the Efficiency Roadmap process, and how to implement it in the three primary phases of a small business's life cycle.

5

The Art of Business: Meet Your New Canvas

Everyone has a plan,
till they get punched in the mouth.
—Mike Tyson (World Champion Boxer)

We spent the first four chapters of this book talking about what you *shouldn't* be doing as a small-business CEO, and explaining precisely whom you should bring onto your team to do all those things that you shouldn't DIY. But aside from teambuilding, we haven't said one word about the responsibilities of the small-business CEO.

That was for a good reason. We had to get you out of the DIY mindset in order to free up your most precious resource, which is, of course, your time. Having done that, we can now turn to the work that forms your core job description as CEO. Indeed, **what we're about to do will fundamentally change the way you think about your business, and yourself in relation to it.**

Think back to the moment you decided to start your business. You had a particular area of expertise—designing websites or making pizzas or practicing law—that made you want to build a business around that skill. You also had a dream of working for yourself and becoming financially independent, and so you took the leap of setting up your own shop, and you've been trying to make it work ever since.

But there's an important difference between applying your expertise to a job at an existing organization, and bringing that expertise to bear in a new business that you're building from the ground up. As the owner of a small business, executing that one specific task, or providing that one particular service, is no longer your entire job description, and may no longer be in your job description at all. And in that way, founding your own business represented a fundamental career change.

Indeed, **your new job has less to do with your established area of expertise, and everything to do with the creative labor of**

designing a business model that answers two distinct—and often challenging—questions:

1. **CREATE VALUE: How can I create the maximum value possible for my clients?**
2. **CREATE EFFICIENCY: How can I capture the maximum share of that value for myself?**

The moment you struck out on your own and set up shop as a small-business owner, your role shifted from skilled technician to a chief executive who is responsible for answering these questions. Of course, plenty of small-business owners have never *explicitly* thought about these questions; instead, they try to answer them implicitly, by establishing a business they fervently hope will create value for their customers, while also bringing in enough money to fund payroll and make a profit too.

But as you now know, the vast majority of start-ups fail. And you'll improve your chances for success exponentially if you directly answer these two key questions and then focus on building your business on that foundation.

To understand precisely what I mean, imagine for a second that you're in the market for a new couch. As a prospective couch buyer, you're concerned with just a few questions: How much is it going to cost me? How will this new couch look in my living room? Is it going to be comfortable and durable?

At the same time, you're absolutely *not* concerned with things like the number of hours a craftsman spent designing and fabricating the couch, or how many alternate patterns and fabrics that craftsman considered and discarded before settling on the final design. That just doesn't make a difference to you.

In other words, you have just a couple needs you're looking to address with this purchase. One is functional: You need a comfortable place to sit. Another is aesthetic: You want it to look good (or at least, decent). A third is social: Your friends and family are going to visit your home and see this couch, thus on some level, you want it to match your personality and social status. Of course, you're not actually thinking in these terms as you shop for a new couch, but nevertheless, you're trying to meet these various needs, and do so within your budget. Ultimately, the couch you choose will be the one that best satisfies your needs relative to its price tag.

Now consider all the couch companies vying for your business. The winner will be the one that is most successful at the following:

1. Understanding your needs, and thus providing a couch with that perfect blend of comfort and aesthetic appeal; and
2. Controlling back-end expenses such that the cost to produce the couch is less than the price you're willing to pay for it.

The company that succeeds at those two things is likely well on its way to becoming a highly successful furniture company (think IKEA). Meanwhile, **the majority of companies won't make it for two key reasons:**

1. **Failure to understand customers' needs.** That might mean, for instance, producing a couch that sacrifices comfort for aesthetics, or the other way around.
2. **Failure to create value for customers over and above the price.** Even if a company produces a couch with the perfect blend of comfort and looks, that's irrelevant if the finished product costs more than you're willing to pay.

Since you've likely seen plenty of ugly or overpriced couches in your day, it's probably not too difficult for you to imagine that many furniture companies have made these mistakes. The underlying reasons aren't hard to imagine, either. Maybe they never spent enough time trying to understand their market. Maybe their manufacturing operations were just inefficient.

But there might be other reasons that are more complex. Consider an ambitious entrepreneur who sets out to design the "perfect" couch. He may take years developing a couch he believes will set a new standard in terms of both beauty and comfort. But after all those years of R&D, let's say the cost of actually manufacturing that perfect couch is $100,000. The target customer may well think it's the best couch out there but she sure won't be shelling out a hundred grand for a couch any time soon. That entrepreneur is on the fast track to bankruptcy *even though* he succeeded at designing a great product.

It might seem strange that we're spending all this time talking about couches, but there's an important nugget of wisdom here. **The difference between a successful business and one that files for bankruptcy isn't so much that one makes a good product and the other one doesn't. Instead, the one that succeeds is the one that's asking the right *customer-centric* questions about what makes a product "good."** Any given product or service has value *only to the extent that it addresses a customer's need,* and does so at a price that's equal to, or less than, that customer's willingness to pay.

In other words, your product is a means to an end; it's a means of satisfying your customers' needs or wants. And because it's a means to an end, it's important to recognize that **your product**

is *not* the core of what you do. What *is* the core of what you do? Your business model.

So now it's time to map out precisely what that business model is. To do so, we'll use a process that's dramatically different from the classic (and tedious) task of writing a formal business plan.

You need a plan—just not a "business plan."

We spent enough time in the first chapters of this book for you to know that you shouldn't be doing tasks you consider boring. Because of the efficiency of passion, you'll do a great job on the stuff you love, and a not-so-good job on anything that bores you to tears. And that's one of a couple reasons why **we're not going to waste time writing a hundred-page business plan that's dry as toast and has little or no practical value for the way your business operates in the real world.**

That type of formal business plan actually rose to prominence with the modern-day large corporation. For a corporation, the business plan is mainly an internally facing document that formalizes the vision of the chief executive and brings hundreds or even thousands of employees to a shared understanding, so they're literally on the same page. It lays out relevant data in a host of areas, from market scope to target customer to internal procedures. In other words, this kind of classic business plan states known facts about the company's market: The customer segments are known; the cost structure is known; the sales and marketing procedures are known, and so on.

None of that applies to your small business. As author, serial entrepreneur, and academician Steve Blank likes to say in regard to start-ups, "The unique people who need a five-year business plan are venture capitalists and [the] Soviet Union."

There are still plenty of people out there who will tell you that you need a standard business plan, but they're wrong. Your small business doesn't operate like a miniature version of a large corporation, so you shouldn't pretend it does.

And yet you still need a plan. In fact, developing and maintaining a laser focus on your business model—the essence of a business plan—should be the absolute core of what you do as a small-business CEO. It's critical to your company's survival.

And that's why you've got your Business Model Canvas. Your new best friend.

The Business Model Canvas

We're going to draft a Business Model Canvas for your small business in about fifteen minutes, and then, over time, we're going to refine that canvas in a process that involves scientific experimentation, iterative learning, and measured progress driven by customer feedback.

You might be saying to yourself, *"Fifteen minutes?* This guy is full of it!"

But the Business Model Canvas isn't some hokey idea I've ginned up to avoid the arduous process of writing a traditional business plan. In fact, there's a revolution afoot in the way that experts—from Silicon Valley to elite MBA programs—think about start-ups and business strategy. There's a growing rejection of the formal business plan and its underlying assumption that the CEO is all-knowing and therefore capable of dictating a plan that's infallible and should be followed to the letter. This new movement has sought ways to apply scientific discovery to business development, deploying an approach of continuous learning that involves testing hypotheses and listening to customers.

This new way of thinking goes by various names. *The Lean Startup,* a book by Eric Ries, takes its title from the "Lean Manufacturing" revolution pioneered by Toyota. Steve Blank likes to call his approach "The Customer Discovery Method." And the Business Model Canvas itself was developed by theorist and author Alexander Osterwalder, with the help of 470 cocreators. Regardless of name, the point of this new approach is to take some of the guesswork out of starting and running a business, and instead, to turn it into more of a science.

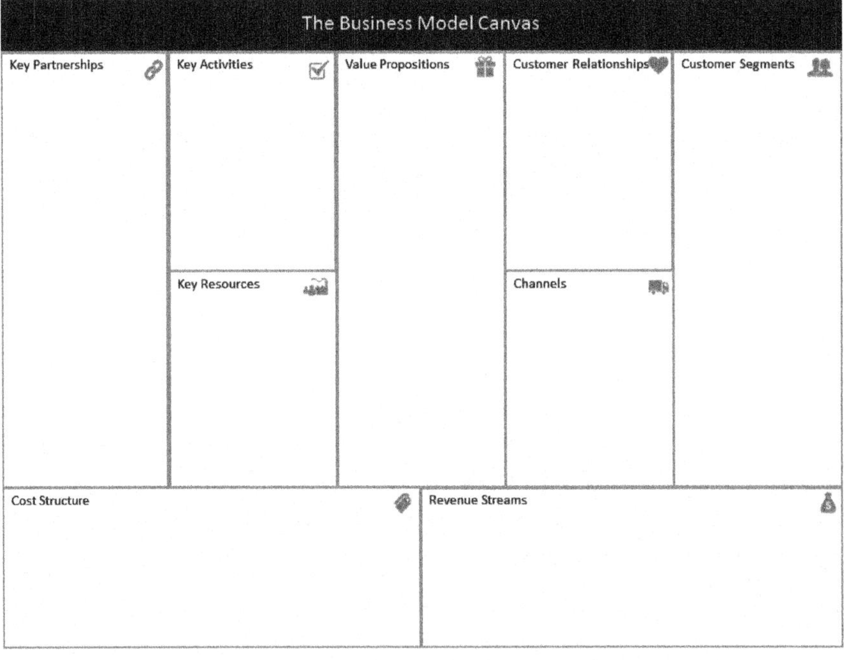

The power of the Business Model Canvas lies in its simplicity and flexibility. In essence, it's an effort to boil down a formal business plan—one that used to require dozens, if not hundreds, of pages of static text—into a malleable single-page document (plus sticky notes) that allows all key stakeholders to see and visualize the business model at a single glance. Then it's easily modified as new information comes to light. The point is to get you to look at your business in entirely new ways, to ask new questions, and to discover new realities.

When you decided to start your own business, you were trying to solve a central *problem*. Maybe that problem was the need to make a living or the desire to be your own boss. So you developed a *hypothesis*—just a fancy word for a guess—about the best way to solve that problem through establishing your own business. For example, if you were good at tending bar, you decided to start your own bar as the best means to solve your money/independence problem. Well, that was a hypothesis—a guess—that starting a bar was the best solution to your problem.

And that hypothesis, in turn, relied on a ton of other hypotheses you may or may not have articulated at the time. To name just a few, you were assuming: (1) There is sufficient market demand to support another bar in your area; (2) you have access to sufficient resources to open a bar when and where you want to open it; (3) you will be able to find, keep, and grow a customer base; and (4) you will be able to charge sufficiently high prices, to a sufficiently large customer base, to turn a profit after paying incurred expenses. Those are just a few of the implicit assumptions.

And those might be perfectly reasonable guesses to make as you start out. But since you've never actually tried opening a bar at this particular moment in this particular neighborhood, you can't be certain you're right about any of those hypotheses.

And **although you have a clear vision for how your business is going to look and operate when you first open your doors, the *vast* majority of the time, the real world looks quite different. To**

quote Mike Tyson, "Everyone has a plan till they get punched in the mouth." Or, as Steve Blank likes to paraphrase, "No business plan survives first contact with a customer."

So while we know you need some kind of a plan for your business, what you really need is something that's designed for experimentation, to test all those guesses and then eventually turn them into fact. You need a tool that allows you to see all the component parts of the plan working in concert with one another, and, in so doing, facilitates building a business that operates like a well-oiled machine.

That tool is the Business Model Canvas—and I say that not as a guess, but after having experimented with lots of small businesses through my work at Agents of Efficiency and in companies I've run myself. I've taken many small-business owners through a step-by-step process that's the path to a viable business and a prosperous future. It's a process that begins with the two key questions introduced at the start of this chapter:

1. CREATE VALUE: How can I create the maximum value possible for my clients?
2. CREATE EFFICIENCY: How can I capture the maximum share of that value for myself?

The first question is about creating value for your customer, and the second is about doing so efficiently. The Business Model Canvas is designed so you see your business through that lens, with the left side of the canvas focusing on efficiency, and the right side, on value.

We're now going to delve into the components of each side of the canvas, from your Value Proposition all the way

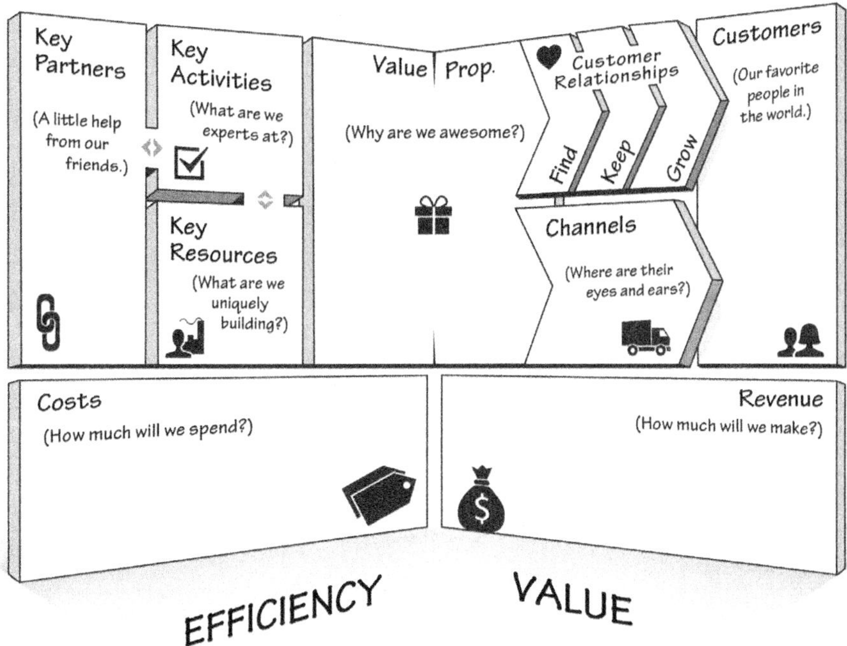

to Cost Structure and Revenue Stream, so you can draft the first canvas for *your* small business. Feeling bold? **Head over to BMC.WeDoBoring.com and download a free digital Business Model Canvas template to play with as you read on.** That's all you need to start making your business smarter and more efficient than it's ever been.

Value Proposition(s)

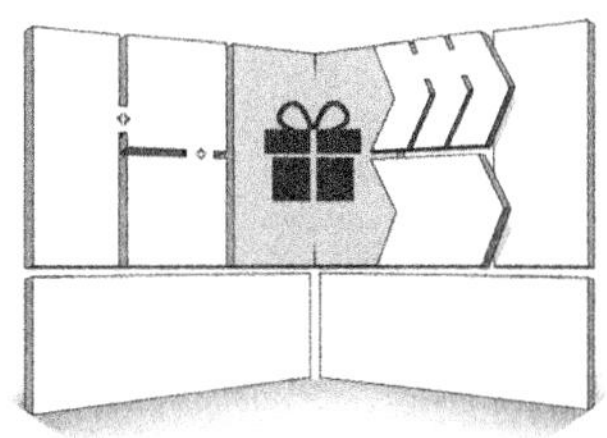

Begin your Business Model Canvas with the section that sits right in the middle: Value Proposition. It's in the middle of the canvas because it's the absolute core of your business; it's the reason your business exists. Everything else leads into, and follows from, the value proposition.

That might sound obvious, but consider this little-known fact. A couple years ago, research emerged on the most common reasons start-ups fail. The top reason? It wasn't money, as is widely believed. Instead, **the most common reason businesses fail is that they're trying to sell a product nobody wants.** And I'm not just referring to the Darth Vader Chia Pet (after all, who *wouldn't* want one of those). You may be trying to build a pizza shop in a saturated market—a location that simply can't support another pizza shop. Or, if you're a lawyer, maybe there's a desperate need for more customs and international trade attorneys, but no demand for another general practitioner who does a little bit of everything.

So you may be tempted to fill in the Value Proposition section of your canvas with a sticky note that says the thing your company makes, or the service it provides: "Legal Services," you might want to write; or, simply, "Pizza." But **your product is *not* the core of your business. The core of your business is the value your company brings into this world.** Examples that are relevant to a law firm or a pizza shop include might "peace of mind," "convenience," "quality," or even "social connection."

If this sounds confusing, don't worry. In the next chapter, we're going to go slowly through the process of developing and refining your value proposition to ensure you've got what's called "product-market fit"—meaning, you've got a product that actually satisfies a need or a want, and the target market can support your business. We'll do so because this is the single most important part of the process, and a guess isn't good enough. Guessing about value proposition is, as we just learned, the most common reason businesses fail: because they guessed wrong and learned the hard way that no one wanted their product.

Pleasure or Pain?

As you're thinking through your business's value proposition, you should be asking yourself: What specific pain points am I alleviating for my customer? Or, alternatively, what specific pleasure am I helping them to experience?

For example, humans are social animals, and we have a basic need for community and to feel connected to others. These are pleasures that Facebook, for instance, provides as its core value proposition. But along our life's path, we also hit an untold number pain points: There's the frustration of commuting home from work and the drudgery of doing laundry, among many others.

While there are exceptions to every rule, it's worth noting that the market for alleviating pain tends to be significantly larger than the market for providing pleasure. Put another way, people are much quicker to invest in aspirin than in vitamins.

Customer Segments

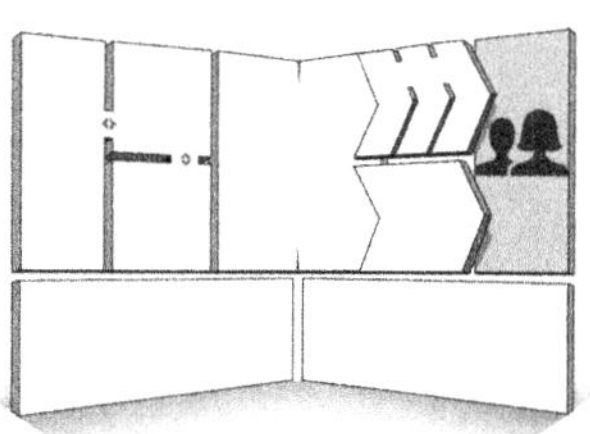

Of course, the concept of "value" is subjective; that is, one person's trash is another person's treasure. So you can't establish your company's core value proposition unless you know who, exactly, will be judging that value. That's why the second part of the Business Model Canvas that requires your attention is "Customer Segments."

The more precise you can be in knowing who your customers are, the better. Ideally, you should be able to draw a picture of your customer archetype: their age, gender, where they live, and so on.

Or perhaps your customers are businesses. If so, you've still got to go through the same line of questioning, since businesses are just made of people. Precisely whom are you trying to serve within these target businesses? Does that person also have the power to write your company a check? If not, maybe you need to bifurcate your business model—the way Facebook does—to address your two customer segments. In Facebook's case, the users who connect with friends and find entertainment on the site do so for free. The customers who actually *pay* Facebook are the businesses trying to reach those users through advertisements.

Regardless of how many customer segments you may have, the goal is to get as specific as possible. And, as was true with the value proposition, the information in this area of the canvas is too important to leave to guesswork. So we'll talk a lot in the next chapter about how to test your hypotheses and turn them into fact. We're also going to talk about the value proposition together with the customer segments, because one without the other has little meaning. When your value proposition fits perfectly with a need or a pain point for your specific customer segment, you've got product-market fit. That's the foundation upon which successful companies are built.

Channels

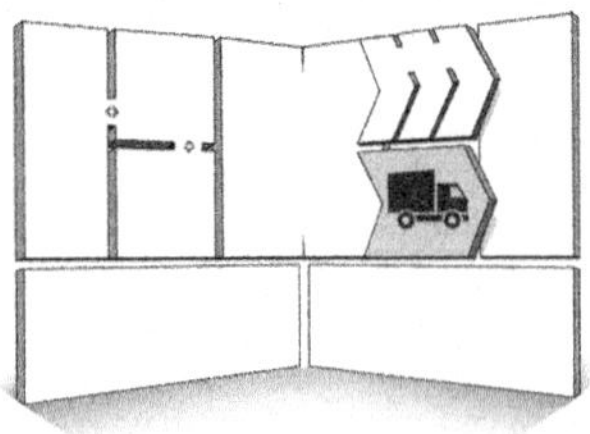

Logistically speaking, how do you actually *deliver* your value proposition to your customers? A physical storefront? A truck? A website or mobile app? This is the next section of the Business Model Canvas: your distribution Channels.

Your answer will have all sorts of implications for the type of business you're building, including for your Cost Structure on the left side of your canvas, and your Customer Relationships on the right.

Customer Relationships

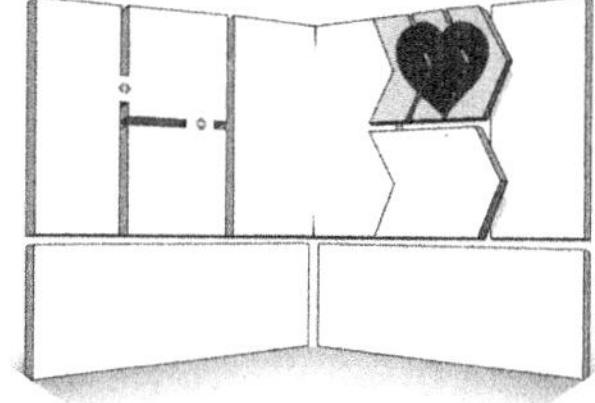

How do you plan to attract customers, keep them, and then grow your customer base?

The Customer Relationships part of the Business Model Canvas is all about sales and marketing: How will customers find out about you? What will get them out of their routine and convince them they should part with their precious money in order to try your unfamiliar product?

Then there's the question of keeping customers once you've attracted them. For this question, most small-business owners think *customer service.* That may be one of your sticky notes for this section of the canvas, and that's great. We'll explore the power of customer service in depth in Chapter Twelve, and its limitations in Chapter Fifteen. But for now, let's just note that it's far from the only way to keep customers coming back again and again. Other strategies for retaining customers include things like "habit" or "high switching costs." For example, have you ever gotten frustrated with your bank, but then started thinking about all the time and energy it would take to switch to a different one? Switching is a painful process, and the banks love it that way! Those high switching costs are at least as central to their model for keeping customers as customer service is, if not more so.

Then there's the question of growth: Once you've got an initial group of customers, how will you grow that base in order to expand your business? Will you just upsell more features, products, and services in order to extract more money from your existing customers? Can you get customers to refer you to their friends? There are lots of possible answers. What's right for your business?

Revenue Streams

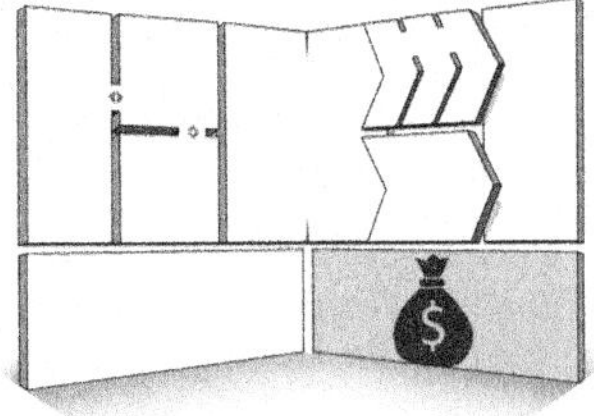

That brings us to the last item on the right side—the *value* side—of your Business Model Canvas: Revenue Streams. This is where you make money. And, hopefully, with your Value Proposition and Customer Segments already on your canvas, this part is fairly clear.

Of course, it may not be the case that *all* of your customer segments are going to hand over money. We just talked about Facebook's bifurcated model, in which users play on the site for free while businesses fork over tons of money to place ads. Similarly, a nonprofit organization may bifurcate its customer segments into the group it plans on helping, and its prospective donors. Or perhaps you can convince the federal government that your business provides a social good, and thus land a government contract or grant. All of these represent different, and perfectly viable, types of revenue streams.

Any way you slice it, though, at least one of your customer segments needs to hand you money. How much, and how they get it to you, goes on sticky notes in this area of the canvas.

And now that you've mapped out Revenue Streams, we've nailed down all the components of the right side of your Business Model Canvas. In other words, we've established the core value your business exists to provide. Thus, we've answered the first of our two key questions: *How can I create the maximum value possible for my clients?*

Now we'll turn to the left side of the canvas.

Key Activities

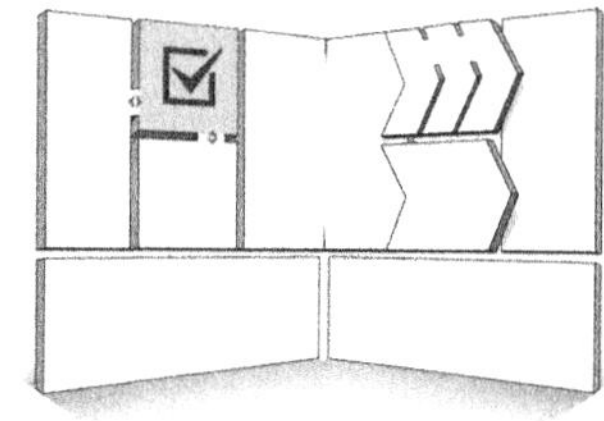

The left side of the canvas is focused on the second of our two key questions: *How can I capture the maximum share of that value for myself?*

We begin to answer that question by taking a close look at Key Activities. That is, **what are the most important activities your team needs to expertly perform in order to create the value your company exists to provide?**

Did you catch that? These are the activities *your team* needs to excel at—not *you!* I make that distinction because this segment of the business model tends to be where most small-business owners spend their time, to the detriment of their company's profitability, their own happiness, and their target customer. **This part of the canvas is what tends to trap small-business owners in the DIY mindset we talked about in Part I of this book. The Business Model Canvas is the small-business owner's road map out of the DIY trap.**

The instinct for many small-business owners is to lump too many activities into this segment of their canvas, and then to perform all those activities internally and on a DIY basis. Starved of the time and space they need to be able to see their business model in its entirety, they lose sight of the fact that **key activities are not the business; the business model is the business.**

Then, lost in the weeds of these key activities, business owners start to feel trapped. They begin spinning their wheels working *in* the business, without ever having time to work *on* the business. The result is waste and inefficiency, while the quality of the value proposition suffers. So **in this area of your Business Model Canvas, we're aiming to hone in on that powerful three-word business plan we first introduced in Chapter Two:**

Do less, better.

What is the *one thing* your company can do better than any of its competitors? (OK, maybe two things—sometimes.) Are you fundamentally a delivery company that exists to get physical goods into the hands of your customers as conveniently as possible? Are you in a problem-solving business like consulting? Are you in a production business—that is, actually making something, either the price or the quality of which is your core value? These are the questions that help you to hone in on the one key activity that's truly essential to your business model.

There are also plenty of activities that don't need to be listed in the Key Activities area of the Business Model Canvas. Bookkeeping and accounting should never be listed here—unless, of course, you're an accounting firm. Every small business needs to maintain good books; that's why you have an outsourced CFO. But don't for a second confuse the importance of that particular back-office task with the key activities that your in-house team *must* become *expert* at in order to make your business model work.

The next three chapters are, in part, devoted to helping you identify which Key Activities rightly belong here, and which don't.

And for the small-business owner who finds himself in the DIY trap, we'll show you pathways out—by harnessing the power of the Key Partners and Key Resources areas of your canvas, among other strategies.

Key Partners

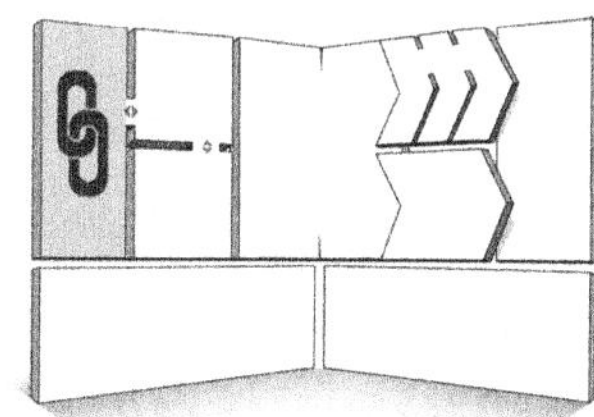

Our next stop in our journey through the Business Model Canvas is Key Partners. This is a powerful area, especially for small businesses that are outmatched in scale by larger competitors.

The potential gain from forming strong partnerships goes unappreciated far too often. As we discussed in Chapter Three, many small-business owners fall into the DIY trap precisely because they envision themselves all alone in their journey—as if on a deserted island—and flail as they try to handle every aspect of the business themselves. Well, it's precisely because small businesses lack size and capital that partnerships are at least as essential as they are for large companies.

It's just like we discussed back in Chapter One: You shouldn't build your own calculator. You've got to rely on the expertise of others in order to build a viable business. So what are the key partnerships you need to propel your business beyond the constraints of your limited cash flow?

It's also the case that the types of partnerships your business may need to survive in its first year may be very different from the ones it will need to thrive in its tenth. And there may be some activities that get moved from the Key Activities area of your canvas to your Key Partnerships area, and then back again.

However this process plays out for your business, remember that partnerships are a powerful, and often overlooked, dimension of the business model—one you can harness both to escape the DIY trap and to develop ambitious plans for the future of your company.

Key Resources

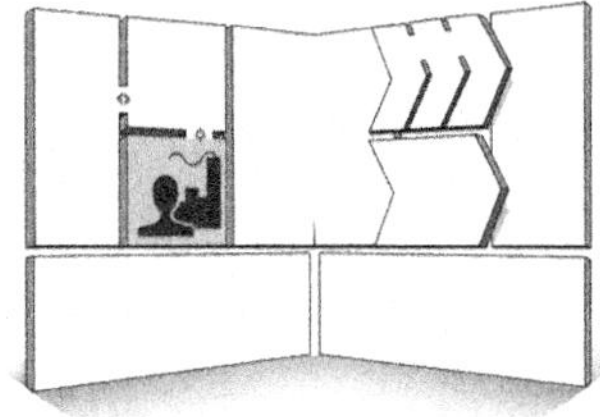

They Key Resources area of the Business Model Canvas is another that often goes underappreciated, and can often serve as a road out of the DIY trap as well.

Back in Chapter One we talked about the start-up capital you didn't know you had: your time. In the next chapters, we're going to explore that idea in more detail, along with the concept of uncovering hidden resources that exist off your balance sheet. For now, it's worth thinking long and hard about the key resources of your business, including trying to identify what resources you might be taking for granted. Ultimately, what are the essential resources that your business model relies upon in order to deliver its core product? What key assets (equipment, buildings, technology) do you need? How much capital do you need? Do you need a line of credit?

Earlier in this chapter I mentioned a study that found that the number-one reason start-ups fail is a lack of product-market fit. What's the second most common reason? Money. And if you've ever made five trips to Home Depot for a home-improvement plan gone wrong, you know how easy it is to underestimate the cost and time required to complete even the smallest project. So imagine how many entrepreneurs are wrong about the resources required to get their business off the ground. Lots of start-ups shut down simply because they don't have enough runway; that is, they don't have enough cash to sustain operations while they're on their way to becoming profitable. We'll get deeper into the weeds of budgeting in Chapter Thirteen, but for now, just recognize the risks here, and the importance of being honest with yourself about what you need to make your business a success.

Over time, as your business grows and changes, the key resources will too. As you begin to carve out a market niche, you'll start to think about how to outperform competitors: What key resources are necessary for your business to execute its value proposition better than anyone else? Put another way, how can you gain an unfair competitive advantage that will make it difficult for anyone to outcompete you in the future? Is it a powerful brand? Intellectual capital? Unique partner relationships? A powerful database (like Facebook) or algorithm (like Google)? Whatever it is, this portion of your canvas is as key to your company's survival in the long term as it is for making it through year one.

Cost Structure

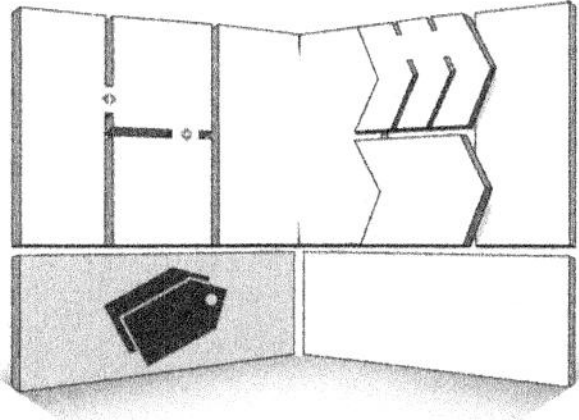

Cost Structure is the very last item on the Business Model Canvas. Add up all costs associated with your activities, partnerships, and resources on the left side of the canvas, and what you've got is the fundamental cost structure for operating your business.

Like Revenue Stream on the right side of the canvas, the Cost Structure is often fairly clear once the rest of the canvas is in place. And just as we said that bookkeeping and other back-office tasks don't belong under Key Activities, the expense associated with internal tasks like bookkeeping don't belong in Cost Structure. They belong in your detailed budget, which we'll get into in Chapter Thirteen. But your canvas exists to make the *big picture* clear and easy to comprehend. So right now, we're only including those costs that are critical to your unique business model.

Once you've got your sticky notes in place to indicate your central costs, you can now step back and look at the overall business model. To the extent that your Cost Structure on the left is less than Revenue Streams on the right, you have yourself a business! To the extent that it's not, you don't.

As we move forward, the goal will be to look at the entire canvas holistically, and to find new and creative ways to grow your Revenue Streams while also, ideally, shrinking the Cost Structure.

The Efficiency Roadmap

In the next three chapters, we're going to dig into the Business Model Canvas in greater detail, and walk through the Efficiency Roadmap process that I use at Agents of Efficiency. It's a process that both liberates small-business owners from the DIY trap *and* helps them to realize the maximum potential for their business.

6

Start: When Slow Is Fast

Wisely and slow. They stumble that run fast.

—William Shakespeare

(English Playwright, 1564–1616)

Imagine you're on a ship in the middle of the ocean. It's the middle of the night, and you wake to the sound of the fire alarm. A red warning light on the ceiling is flashing. You feel a paralyzing terror as you picture the ship ablaze in water that's cold enough to cause hypothermia in minutes.

I wish this were only a hypothetical. Unfortunately, it actually happened to me.

I was on a commercial ship and it was my job to be the first line of defense—meaning, I was the one who had to don firefighting gear and head to the engine room. My hands shook wildly as I tried to pull on my fire-retardant pants. But an experienced sailor was there with me, and he saw my panic as I tried to dress.

"Slow is fast," he said, his voice calm. "Slow is fast."

Thanks to him, I slowed down and was able to get the suit on. And, as you can see, I lived to tell the story.

When I became an entrepreneur years later, I realized that the same wisdom, "slow is fast," applies to the early stages of building a business. That might sound paradoxical. It's certainly counterintuitive. And it runs contrary to the advice I hear far too often from my friends in Silicon Valley, who, inspired by Nike's *Just Do It* motto, sometimes preach the idea of "failing fast." Budding entrepreneurs are typically passionate about their new venture—which is, of course, a great thing—but that passion and excitement often translates into dangerous haste.

When you're a small business entering a market crowded with established competitors, slow is *definitely* fast. That is, **shortcutting the strategy development for your fledgling business is almost never a recipe for success.**

There's another way, and it's far more likely to produce a fruitful business model. **The alternative to the standard entrepreneurial rush is a process in which the new CEO tests the market and tweaks the business model in order to establish product-market fit *before* serving a single customer.**

Because, while learning from your mistakes is some of the best education out there, it's also some of the most expensive. Investing yourself in preliminary strategy development will save you time, headaches, and a ton of money.

At Agents of Efficiency, we guide entrepreneurs through the **Efficiency Roadmap** process: a method for building a business model that nails product-market fit, and does so by starting out slowly. In this and subsequent chapters, I'm going to take you through this process by following an entrepreneur named Sue on her journey of starting her own bagel business.

We'll assume Sue has read this book up to this chapter, and that she's already found an expert outsourced COO to guide her through the Efficiency Roadmap process beginning on day one, that is, before she spends a dime on her new business. But even with that solid foundation, Sue will *still* fall into a DIY trap.

Sue's Bagels

Sue was raised in northeastern New Jersey, where people love their bagels. She loves them too, and has a great bagel recipe that has been passed down through her family. Sue now lives in Pennsylvania, and she has discovered that good bagels are hard to find. An idea comes to her, and she just can't shake it: "I should start my own bagel shop!"

So Sue does the first thing that many budding entrepreneurs do: She looks for a storefront. It doesn't take long for her to find the perfect location. It's several miles from the nearest competing bagel shop and in a well-trafficked area. She starts calculating the cost: annual rent plus all the equipment she's going to have to buy, as well as the host of other expenses she'll incur just to open the shop. It's going to take all of her savings, plus a second mortgage on her home, not to mention borrowing from friends and family. She even meets with a half-dozen banks about a Small Business Administration loan.

It's a heck of a gamble. Statistics vary on the rate at which start-ups fail, and it varies by industry, but for the restaurant industry specifically, there's about a 60 percent chance a new venture will fail in the first three years.[14] If that happened to Sue, it would probably leave her bankrupt. That's terrifying.

Yet the process of starting a new business doesn't have to be nearly as scary and uncertain as it seems to Sue, and as it is for most entrepreneurs. Let's take a look at how Sue's Bagels can use the "slow is fast" wisdom, not only to beat the odds and *survive*, but also to *thrive*, for many years to come.

The Small-Business ~~Owner~~ Visionary

Sue's excitement for her new venture has pulled her into the details: finding a storefront, researching industrial kitchen equipment, calculating costs. But her outsourced COO suggests that Sue step back for a moment. In fact, she suggests Sue think of herself not so much as a soon-to-be small-business *owner*, but rather as a visionary.

"A visionary?" asks Sue, wrinkling her brow.

That's the last thing she has ever considered herself. But Sue's job as the CEO of a budding enterprise *is* to be a visionary; that is, it's her job to lay out a vision for the new company that will be sustainable, profitable, and predictable. And doing so begins with the first of the two key questions introduced in the last chapter:

1. **CREATE VALUE: How can I create the maximum value possible for my clients?**
2. CREATE EFFICIENCY: How can I capture the maximum share of that value for myself?

Most small-business owners have the same instinct Sue did: to gloss over the visioning and jump right into logistics. But **you can't do the logistics of your business until you know precisely what your business is. And knowing *that* means identifying your target customer and spelling out exactly how your product meets that customer's need or want, in a way that's dramatically better than the current options.** The more precise you can be, and the more confident you are that you *know* the answers instead of just guessing at them, the greater your chance for success.

Heeding her COO's advice, Sue steps back from logistical issues and focuses on the question of how she'll create maximum value for her customers within the core competency of her new business. Her COO suggested Sue use her Business Model Canvas to do so, and to start by defining her Value Proposition and Customer Segments.

Sue's initial impulse is to define her Value Proposition and Customer Segments broadly and simply. She writes out her Value

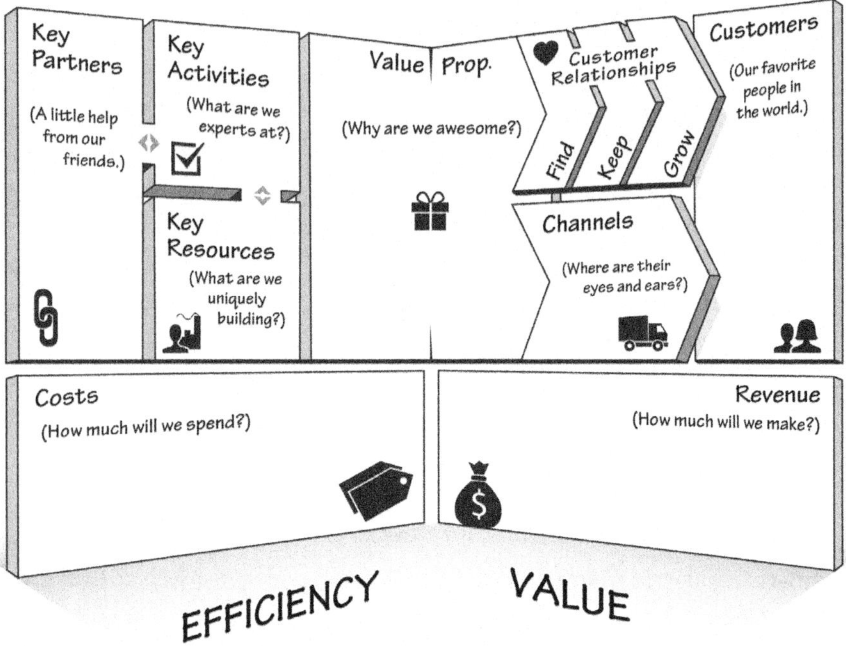

Proposition in simple terms: *I want to sell great bagels*. Sue knows there's an established market for bagels, so she doesn't see much reason to overthink that. Customer Segments seems pretty clear too: *I want to sell great bagels to people who like bagels*. Or, to get really specific, *I want to sell great bagels to people who like bagels and live or work within a five-mile radius of 123 Main Street*. Seems simple enough.

But if Sue wants to beat the odds and succeed in an industry where her chances of failure are at least 60 percent in the first three years, she's going to have to do better than that. Her initial blunder lies in the first two words of her value proposition: "I want." Customers aren't going to hand over their hard-earned money just because Sue wants them to.

But even if she just removes the "I want," her value proposition *still* isn't a slam dunk. Remember from the last chapter: **Your product is *not* your value proposition *or* the core of what you do.**

There are, however, two value propositions embedded in Sue's statement about wanting to sell great bagels to people who live or work within a five-mile radius of 123 Main Street. The first is quality, and the second is convenience.

Value Proposition(s):

- Quality: Sue's dream of opening her own bagel shop began because she knows how to make a *great* bagel, and she's always found the quality of Pennsylvania bagels lacking. In other words, Sue's experience led her to a hypothesis: There are enough people in her surrounding area who want a better bagel and who would be willing to come into her shop regularly to spend their money on great bagels.

- Convenience: Sue's instinct to open a storefront in her local area rests on the idea that it's a convenient location for would-be bagel consumers.

Now that she's teased out the value propositions of value and convenience, Sue has a little more insight into the core of her business than she did when she merely *said* she would sell great bagels. In fact, these value propositions help her to visualize her target customer more clearly. Her core customer segment will be local, discerning consumers.

Customer Segments:

- Local: Sue's vision is to sell bagels at a physical storefront. This is far from the only way to get bagels into the hands of customers, and may not be the ideal channel for Sue, but that's her initial plan.

- Discerning: Sue's core value proposition of quality relies on the hypothesis that she can make a better-tasting bagel than what's currently available locally, *and* that there's a sufficient number of local residents who will recognize and value that quality enough to pay for her bagels over the other options available to them. It's a risky hypothesis. What if Pennsylvanians are just too obsessed with cheesesteaks to care about bagels, or even to know the difference between a good one and a bad one? But, for now, this is Sue's hypothesis.

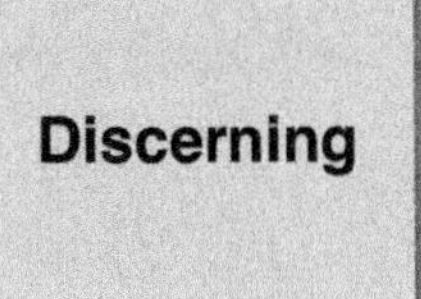

- Consumers: Sue's statement that she wants to sell bagels to "people who live or work within a five-mile radius of 123 Main Street" means she's going to sell directly to consumers. This isn't her only option; she could sell to businesses or wholesalers. But her starting hypothesis is that selling directly to consumers through a physical store is the best means of getting the largest number of bagels into the hands of as many people as possible.

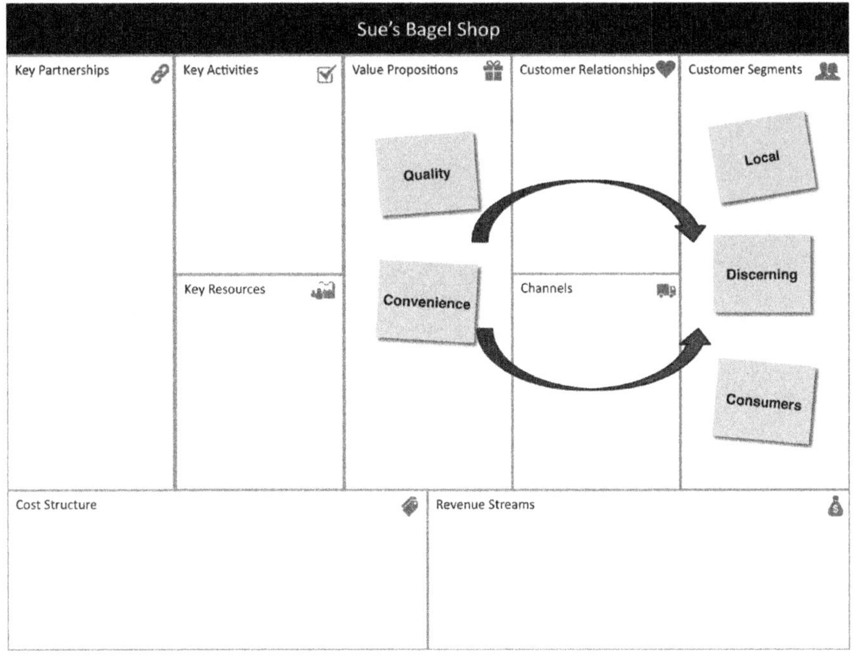

With her core Value Propositions and Customer Segments in place, Sue sets about filling in the other areas of the canvas. "Channels" is simple: She's got her storefront, and she plans on handing bagels directly to her customers across a counter. It doesn't get any simpler than that. For "Customer Relationships," the question of how to find, keep, and grow her customer base, Sue decides she'll use good signage to attract customers and great customer service to keep them, and that she'll upsell (adding lox, freshly squeezed orange juice, and other amenities to her menu) in order to grow the amount of money each customer puts into her register.

It doesn't take much longer for Sue to complete the rest of her Business Model Canvas. "Revenue Stream" is easy (money from selling bagels, duh!).

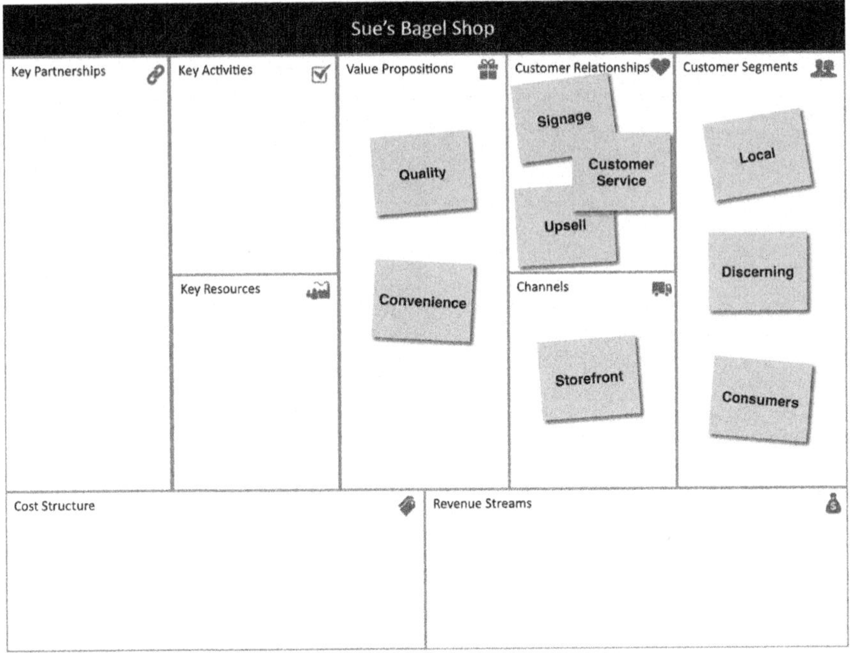

But what about "Key Resources" and "Key Partnerships"? These are harder. After thinking about it for a while, she decides her most important resources are her family recipe and her storefront. As for partners, she has a lightbulb moment and realizes that of course she's not going to be making her own flour or cream cheese or orange juice, so her suppliers are essential to her business model.

She turns to "Key Activities." That's pretty easy. Making bagels is at the top of the list, followed by serving customers.

With all of that in place, the final area of her canvas, "Cost Structure," is straightforward. It's the sum total of rent, equipment, labor, and all the supplies for making the bagels (which is simply called "COGS," or "Cost of Goods Sold," in accounting speak).

And just like that, Sue finishes her first Business Model Canvas.

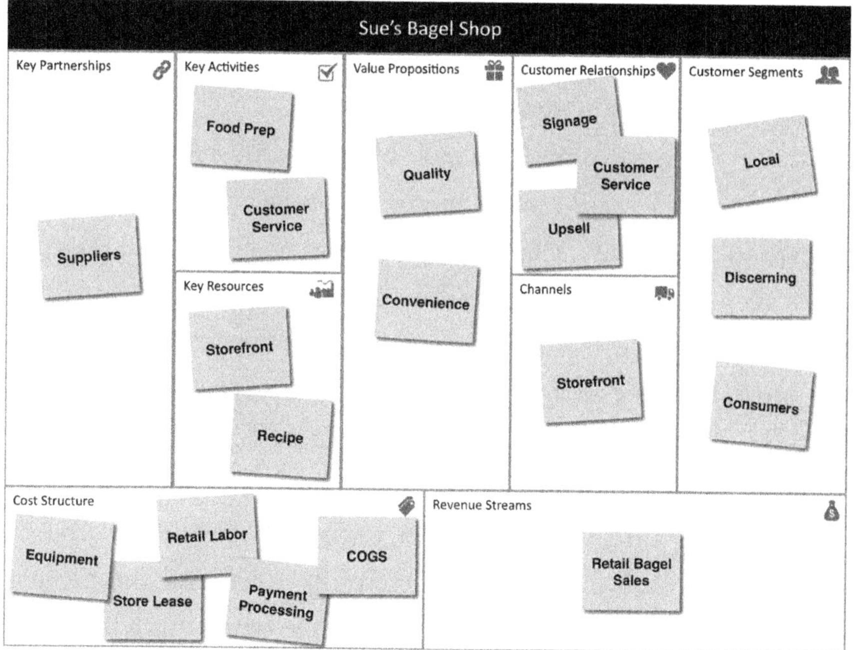

Slow Is Fast: Doing the Numbers

Sue is feeling really happy with her Business Model Canvas and her plans for moving forward. And thanks to the guidance from her COO, she's really done her homework on all the key numbers for launching and maintaining this business.

She knows, for instance, that she'll need to commit about $50,000 to secure a three-month lease for the 1,400-square-foot property she wants at 123 Main Street, and another $100,000 to renovate that space for her needs. Equipment to make the bagels and to store refrigerated goods will set her back $150,000. She knows she has to set aside about $50,000 to cover all the administrative, regulatory, and legal fees. And she assumes she'll probably need about $50,000 to pay her personal bills and keep the lights on at home between the time she quits her job and when she can actually start drawing a salary. As she moves forward, there will also be the costs of labor and supplies.

Then there's the revenue side of things. By her math, she'll need just over $5,000 a week in gross sales to break even, $6,000 weekly to pull in about $50,000 in annual profit, and $8,000 per week to pull in $100,000 a year—a magic number because it's just more than she's currently earning at her day job. So, assuming the average customer spends about $20 per visit, Sue needs 250 customers a week to break even, 300 to make $50,000 a year, and 400 to make a cool $100,000.

And how hard can that be? A lousy 400 customers! Sue is confident she has the best bagel recipe in town and the perfect location, and that her Business Model Canvas represents a beautiful plan.

The only problem? Sue's beautiful plan is a surefire recipe for failure. She just doesn't know it yet.

Statistically speaking, Sue has about a 40 percent chance of her bagel shop surviving into year three. More to the point, though, we have *no idea* about the chance of her bringing home $100,000 versus $20,000, or even less.

Sue's situation is similar to that of most entrepreneurs. **Most entrepreneurs choose to push forward despite the uncertainty. Some succeed, and others learn the hard way—after draining their savings and borrowing to the hilt—that their business model just wasn't viable.**

But Sue doesn't need to quit her day job and risk $400,000 to find out if she can make a decent living at her bagel shop. There's a better way.

Slow Is Fast: Hypothesis Testing

Right now, Sue's plan is based on quite a few hypotheses; that is, she's made a bunch of guesses about the market for her product. Specifically, **her business model hinges on a guess that her core value proposition will be exciting to her customer segments, and that she's nailed the "product-market fit."** But those are mere guesses; she doesn't know them for certain.

Even to the extent that Sue's plan includes market research on things like the nationwide appetite for bagels and historic success rates of bagel shops, she still doesn't know much about the market for *her* shop. She isn't opening a nationwide bagel store, nor is she opening a bagel shop in the past, when all the data were collected. Sue is opening a bagel shop at 123 Main Street, this year.

As it turns out, though, it's not that hard to figure out what the bagel market looks like *right now* within a five-mile radius of 123 Main Street. All Sue needs to do is get out of her home office and take a look. So, under the advice of her COO, she does just that.

It's an especially easy task for Sue to scan the local bagel market because she's currently focused only on the people who are already bagel consumers. She sees her potential customer base the way many new entrepreneurs do: as a zero-sum game. She's looking at existing bagel shops and she's asking herself, "How do I capture some of that market for myself?" In fact, that's *not* the only way to build a customer base, and the most successful entrepreneurs tend to *create* new markets rather than just siphoning customers from the competition. But that's how Sue is proceeding for the moment.

So Sue sets out to test her hypothesis about the size of the existing market of local bagel consumers. That sounds difficult, but it turns out to be pretty straightforward. She's already scouted her competition. There are only two dedicated bagel shops that Sue considers competitors. There are also places like grocery stores, gas stations, and Dunkin' Donuts that sell bagels as an add-on to their core offerings. But Sue is focused on the stand-alone bagel shops, so testing her hypothesis about the size of the market is just a matter of making the rounds to see how many customers each of the shops have.

She goes into each of the two shops and buys a bagel, and at each place, she casually inquires about how many customers they get each week. She gets a surprisingly candid response: At each one, the answer is around 300.

"Huh," Sue thinks to herself. "That's not good."

By Sue's math, assuming the average customer spends around $20 per visit, that means each of her competitors is only making about $50,000 per year—and that's the very bottom of the range in which Sue could sustainably maintain her own shop.

"But maybe $20 is conservative," she thinks. "Maybe the average customer is spending more than that?"

So she tests that hypothesis.

She camps out in front of her competitors' stores at various times throughout the week, and watches what the customers buy. It turns out that $20 is about right, on average. Some more, some less, but it's generally in the range of $20.

"Really not good," Sue thinks.

Right now, Sue's fundamental belief is that a sufficient number of people in her local area will recognize and value the quality of her bagels such that they'll buy *her* bagels over the other options available. In other words, Sue has been assuming that the market of "discerning" consumers—those who really care about the quality and taste of a bagel—was big enough for her to carve a place in it.

But now Sue is beginning to worry.

She always knew that competing with places like gas stations and the drive-thru at Dunkin' Donuts would be hard, since the people who buy bagels from those places are more focused on grabbing a quick breakfast than they are on the quality of a bagel. And she knows she can't compete on convenience with a drive-thru. So it's the number of customers at the stand-alone bagel shops that matters to her right now.

But if her two closest and most important competitors only have about 600 customers between them, she figures even if she did really, really well, she could maybe pull half of those customers to her new store. In other words, Sue's *best-case* scenario would be to make only $50,000 a year. And she'd probably be putting two other bagel shops out of business as a result.

All of a sudden, Sue goes from feeling excited about her new business to being scared, and a little sick. She doesn't really want to kill two other small businesses. The zero-sum approach is losing its luster.

Then she has another idea: If her bagels are really the best around, *maybe* she can draw customers from the gas stations and Dunkin' Donuts. That idea intrigues her, so she sets out to test this new hypothesis.

Slow Is Fast: The Insight That Changes Everything

What better way to find out what the customers want than by simply asking them? Sue heads to her local Dunkin' Donuts and strikes up a conversation with everyone who buys a bagel and is willing to spare a minute of his or her time.

At first, her questions are really focused on selling people on the quality of her bagels. She arrives armed with samples (and gives them out discreetly, so the cashier won't notice). And everyone who tastes Sue's bagels says that they are delicious.

But she has a feeling she needs a little more information than that. So she brings in still more samples, and she changes her questions so they are a bit more open-ended. Then she just listens. And she starts to hear people talk about bagels as an easy and portable breakfast. No one says much about quality or taste. Even though every single person says they like her bagels better than the Dunkin' Donuts ones, it also doesn't seem like it is a big deal to anyone. No one seems particularly concerned with the relative quality of the bagels.

Maybe it is a fluke, and she's just talking to a lot of people who don't care one way or another about the taste of a bagel.

So she repeats her experiment a couple more times, alternating which days of the week she does it.

But she gets the same result.

And that is when Sue comes to an incredible realization: Nobody cares!

Whether at Dunkin' Donuts or the gas station, people seem to be buying bagels because it is a convenient breakfast at a convenient stop along their route. At the gas station Sue sees that people have formed a habit of buying gas, getting a cup of coffee, and grabbing a bagel on their way to work. Similar logic applies to people who swing by the Dunkin' Donuts. On top of that, pretty much everyone says that they sometimes buy donuts instead of bagels. The bagels themselves—and their quality and taste—just don't seem to matter.

"How can these people not appreciate good bagels?" Sue thinks to herself, packing samples into her car and heading home. "No one in Jersey would ever stand for the bagels we have here."

But Sue isn't in New Jersey; she is in Pennsylvania. And from the perspective of the local market, her value proposition of providing *high-quality* bagels is an effort to solve a nonexistent problem. Nobody cares.

The Rip Cord Off-ramp

At this stage, Sue could just give up.

She might even consider herself lucky, because she narrowly avoided making a terrible mistake. The "slow is fast" approach has already saved her about $400,000, not to mention years of futile work attempting to build a sustainable business from a bagel shop at 123 Main Street. In fact, a powerful outcome of the Efficiency Roadmap process is having all of this information *before* leaving a secure job and taking on loads of debt.

Knowing what she now knows, Sue could just keep her job and give up her bagel-shop dream.

But Sue isn't ready to give up. In fact, **Sue is just days away from launching her new business. It's a business with the potential to dwarf even the most successful stand-alone bagel shop. And she'll quickly shift gears, from "slow is fast" to "fast is fast."**

7

Grow: When Fast Is Fast

If you are not embarrassed by the first version of your product, you've launched too late.

—Reid Hoffman

(Cofounder and Executive Chairman, LinkedIn)

Sue comes to a sad discovery at the end of the last chapter. She has been pursuing what she'd thought was a fantastic idea: to sell delicious bagels in a market where there are currently none. But that turned out to be a poor business model. Thanks to some market research, Sue has learned that nobody in her neighborhood really cares about the lack of great bagels. Her plan to open a storefront at 123 Main Street was doomed to fail.

After that discovery, she goes home and sits down with her Business Model Canvas. She sees that many of her original assumptions had been wrong.

Even though everyone Sue interviewed said her bagels were delicious, it became clear that taste just isn't enough to get them to change their routine. Opening a physical storefront—with all of the hefty associated costs—just doesn't seem to make sense.

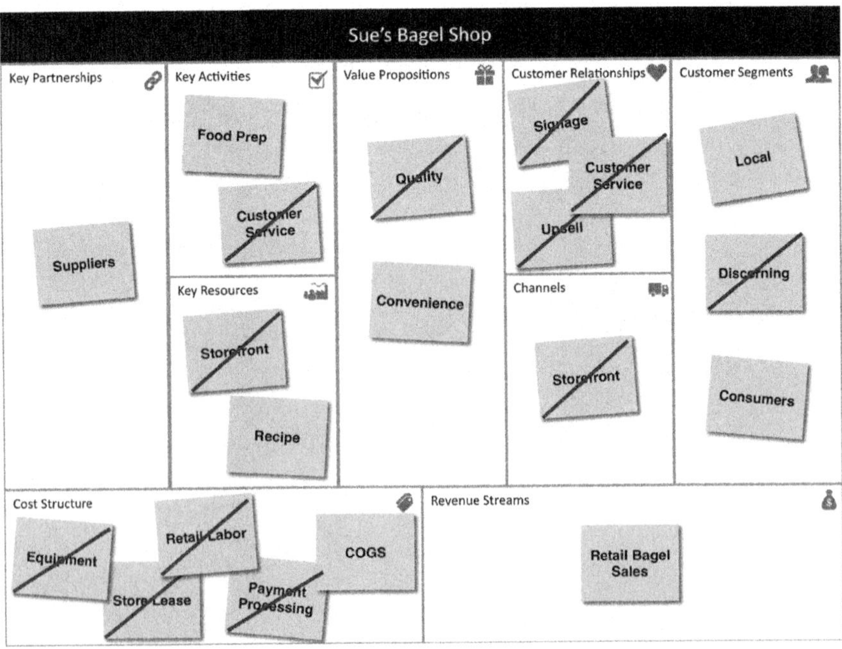

Sue's business model has all but disappeared. She has no Channels—no way to get the bagels into the hands of her customers. She has no means of developing Customer Relationships. Plus, her Key Resources, Key Activities, and Cost Structure have mostly disappeared too. She finds herself with a depressingly empty canvas.

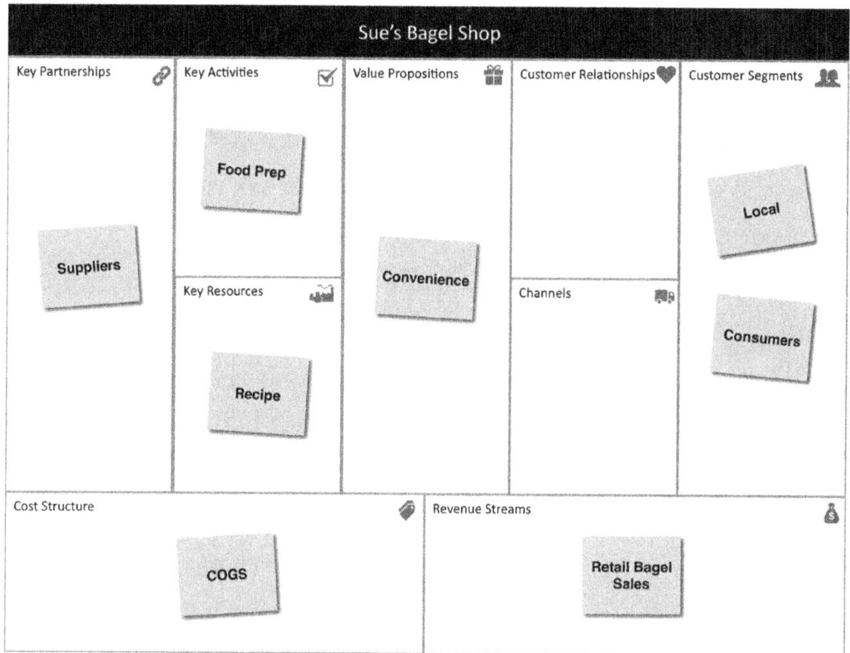

And then it happens.

Sue has the "aha!" moment that she will always remember as the start of her business. Staring her in the face—right at the center of her canvas, shouting for attention—is her core value proposition: convenience.

That's what person after person had told her, one way or another: Convenience and habit are the things that matter most. In the eyes of her customers, nothing could be more valuable than convenience. She hadn't been able to see that initially, since her entire journey had begun as a quest to raise the quality of bagels in Pennsylvania. For months, that had kept her from considering any other value proposition. But Pennsylvanians didn't care about bagel quality; they cared about convenience—and now she sees a way to give it to them.

What could be *even more convenient* than a drive-thru or gas station on the way to work?

Sue is practically giddy with the answer: The only thing more convenient is *not having to make an extra stop!* What if the bagels were just *waiting for her customers* in their break room at work? It can't get any more convenient than that!

Sue doesn't need an expensive storefront, because she can bring her bagels directly to her customers. Not only is that more convenient than a gas station or drive-thru, it is the rare delivery channel that could get people to change their habits. In an instant, Sue realizes *exactly* how she would gain one customer after another after another: One day you're late to work and don't have time for your usual Dunkin' Donuts stop. By ten o'clock you're starving—and lo and behold, a tray of bagels is just sitting there in the break room. You try one, and discover it's delicious. It's better than anything you've *ever* had at Dunkin' Donuts. And all of a sudden, having to make an extra stop every morning on your way to work—for a bagel that's not even that good—seems like, well, too much work.

Sue is so excited that it takes her a few minutes to calm down enough to write the new idea on her canvas. And little does she know, she has just stumbled into one of the most powerful strategies of the lean start-up movement: Sue has herself an MVP.

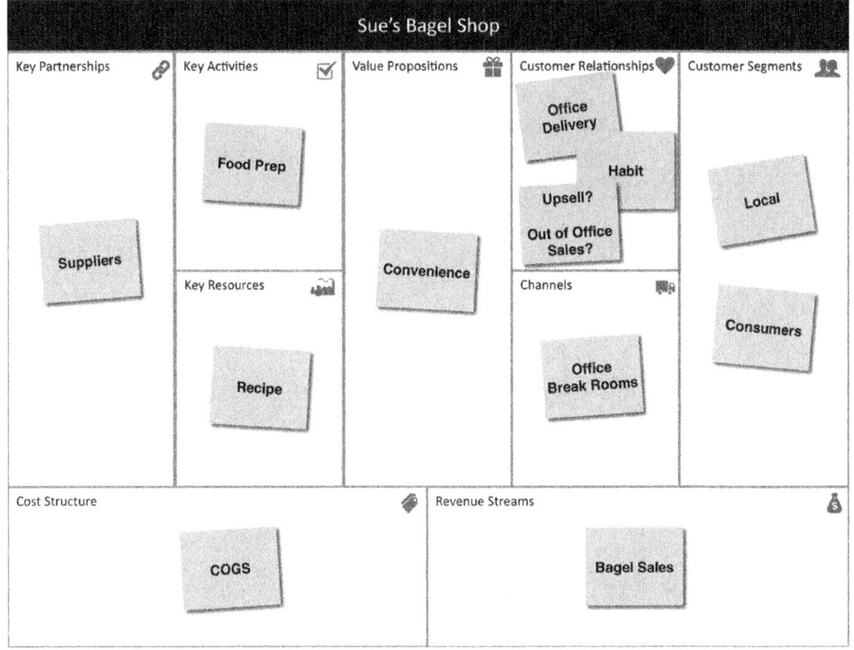

The Minimum Viable Product

In Chapter One we talked about the million-dollar calculator and the fact that LeBron doesn't mow his own lawn. In Chapter Two we talked about the efficiency of passion, while Chapter Three was all about assembling the right team so you can spend your time on actually building your business. All of these concepts are grounded in a single idea: That **there's *one thing* your company exists to do, and you should focus on doing it better than any other business on the planet.**

That runs counter to the instincts of many entrepreneurs who continually add new features and services to their core offerings in an effort to chase what their customers *might* want (or, worse, what the entrepreneurs themselves think is cool). In fact, **what separates successful businesses from failing ones isn't the knowledge of**

which bells and whistles to *add*; it's recognizing which features to *eliminate*. Hence the wisdom behind the Minimum Viable Product (MVP) and the Minimum Viable Service (MVS). **The MVP is the product—and the MVS, the service—that delivers the greatest return on investment for the least amount of risk.**

> Perfection is achieved not when there is nothing more to add, but when there is nothing left to take away.
>
> —Antoine de Saint-Exupéry (French Writer, 1900–1944)

Sue almost took a "more is more" approach to starting her business. She started out with the idea of opening a (costly) storefront, and she had plans to offer amenities like lox and freshly squeezed orange juice. Her reasoning went something like this: "Maybe my customers want lox and OJ and breakfast sandwiches and a million other things on the menu? Let's offer it all and see." If she had done that, she would have failed.

Why? Two primary reasons: cost and lack of focus.

The first reason might be obvious. Every one of those additions to the business model would add to Sue's cost structure. Every ingredient costs money to buy, maintain, and then throw away if the ingredients spoil. And we already know the storefront itself was a huge expense that didn't create value for a customer base focused only on convenience.

What's more, these add-ons to her business model cost heavily in time as well as money. Sue's time, as we know from earlier chapters, is her ultimate nonrenewable resource. If she spends all of it worrying about rent, signage, the recipes and ingredients for a bunch of special menu items, and actually running her shop, she's not spending that time creating value for her customers since not one of those things improves convenience. Sue would have burned money and time while also failing to deliver what the customer actually wanted.

The other reason the "more is more" approach wouldn't have worked for Sue has to do with focus. As soon as Sue tries to do many things instead of just one, she becomes a jack-of-all-trades and master of none.

Happily, Sue recognized all of that before it was too late, and now she has a simple and elegant MVP. With that MVP, she's in a position to launch a business that is laser-focused on what her customers want. What's more, she's in a position to collect a ton of additional data about that customer in a way that will allow her to dramatically improve her business model, and do so at a blistering pace.

That might not sound like a big deal, but in fact, it's astonishingly powerful. Besides promising the greatest ROI with the least amount of risk, **a Minimum Viable Product allows the entrepreneur to collect the greatest volume of feedback from customers with the least amount of effort.** Done right, an MVP can unlock billion-dollar markets.

And that's why we're going to take a very brief detour from Sue and her bagels: to consider one of the greatest MVPs of all time.

Interlude: The Dropbox Story

When the digital-file-sharing company Dropbox first began, it was just two guys and a simple question: "If we can make sharing files across devices easier than anyone else, will customers give it a try?"

They weren't proposing the *best* file-sharing tool *or* the one with the most features. They were only proposing the *simplest*. It's the embodiment of that powerful three-word business plan: Do less, better.

These two guys had a great and simple idea, but the odds were still stacked against them. They planned to enter a market in which they'd be competing with Microsoft, Google, and Apple. Meanwhile, the Dropbox founders were just two guys nobody had ever heard of.

So how did they make their start? With a video that made the new company's value proposition crystal clear: effortless file sharing across a variety of platforms. It was also carefully crafted to attract a techie crowd—in other words, precisely the people who would be the most likely early adopters of such a technology. The video was just three minutes, and it was full of inside jokes that the techie audience loved. Then there was a simple landing page where viewers could log their names and e-mail addresses to become the first wave of Dropbox users.

The two founders launched the video and watched their list grow.

In no time, they had five thousand people, then seventy-five thousand. Boom! No focus groups. No surveys with potentially biasing questions. They had seventy-five thousand people who didn't just *say* they were interested, but who had actually taken an action to *show* they were interested, by putting down their name and e-mail address.

Armed with rock-solid certainty that there was a market for their product, the two founders got to work. But did they build out their own servers and develop a product with a ton of features that would work on every imaginable platform? Nope, they sure didn't. They built an elegant MVP.

Rather than create their own servers, they simply rented space from Amazon, and then built an interface that would allow users to easily move their files onto Amazon's servers, and then back to their devices again. Did it work on every major platform? No. Was it the most secure system in the world? No. Did it have features for collaboration and ways to prevent two people from editing the same file at once? No. But what it *did* do, it did well. It just worked.

Then the two founders listened. Carefully. They collected data from their initial user base to keep improving the product, day by day, week by week.

Customers flocked. In 2008, they had one hundred thousand users. In fifteen months, by January 2010, that number had shot up to over four million. By May 2012, it had reached fifty million, then more than one hundred million, and over two hundred million by the end of 2013.

By the end of 2015, Dropbox was valued at over $10 *billion*.

How did this lean start-up outcompete big-time challengers like Microsoft (SkyDrive and SharePoint Online), Google (Google Drive), and Apple (iCloud)? By maintaining a laser focus on one simple sticky note in the Value Proposition on their Business Model Canvas: "Ease of Use."

To this day, one of Dropbox's biggest competitive advantages is how seamlessly it works across a tremendously wide variety of devices. Over time, Dropbox has expanded to more and more platforms, and has added more and more features, but it's never compromised its core value. It just *works*.

Sue does less, better.

Sue now has an MVP so elegant she needs just two things to launch: bagels and an office break room where she can deliver them.

So she goes into a couple nearby office buildings and talks with a bunch of office managers. She's done a bit of research about how vending-machine arrangements typically work—that's the closest model she can think of to her new idea—and she offers the office managers 20 percent of her net sales in exchange for the opportunity to place her bagels and cash box in their break room. A few of them say no for various reasons, but the vast majority say "Yes!" Sue has the makings of a business!

Now there are just a couple things she has to do before she delivers her first batch of bagels.

First, she has a couple questions about the legality of all this. What are the relevant regulations? Will the health code approve of her making commercial bagels in her home kitchen? Should she form some sort of legal entity to protect her?

She could waste a lot of time on the Internet trying to find the answers, but she read Part I of this book, so she knows that's a poor use of her time. Plus, she has a great COO, who recommends an attorney—someone who will be Sue's very own CLO.

In less than an hour, Sue's CLO gives her a ton of great information. She learns that Pennsylvania's regulations for operating a "dual-use kitchen" are some of the most lenient in the nation. All she needs is a simple baby gate to make sure her dog never sets foot in her kitchen, a health-code inspection from the local inspector, and registration of her company as a "limited food establishment," which costs a measly $35. It's almost too good to be true!

Sue's CLO also suggests something she never would have thought of on her own: a simple contract with the office managers to govern the details of their relationship and to prevent any future headaches. Done!

That new legal agreement also helps her to see that she'd omitted something important from her Business Model Canvas. She makes an addition to Key Partnerships.

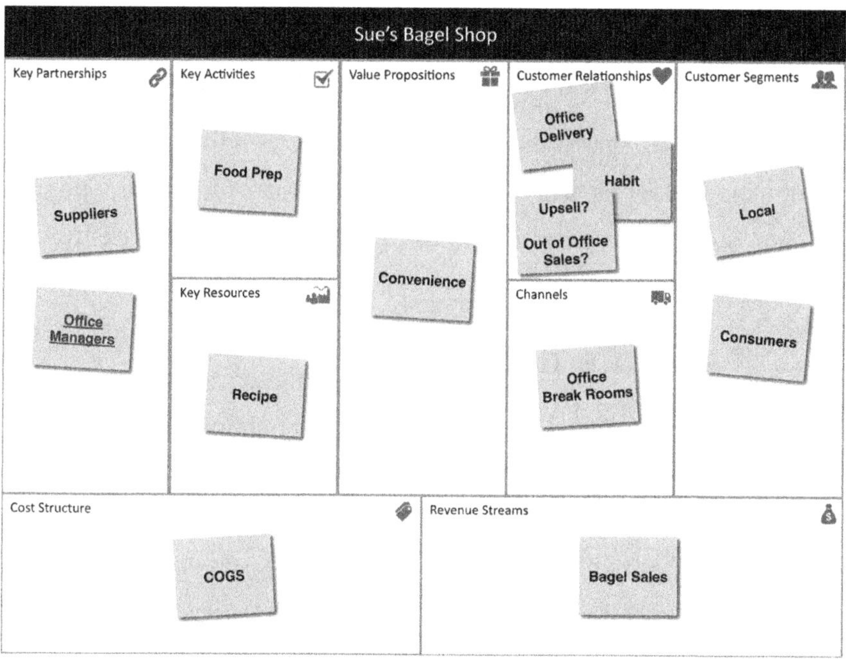

The office managers, of course, are an essential part of her business model. While it is expensive to give them 20 percent of her net profits, it is a heck of a lot cheaper—and far less risky—than retaining a storefront that would have cost $400,000.

In fact, Sue has hardly spent a dime on her new business. She's paid for a few hours of time with her outsourced COO, less than an hour with her CLO, the thirty-five-dollar registration fee, and now all she needs are baking supplies. Meanwhile, she'll soon start bringing in revenue. Practically giddy, and under direction from her COO, Sue hires an outsourced CFO to keep tabs on forthcoming revenue, as well as expenses, and to plan for things like sales tax.

Then she designs a latched box with a slit in the top to serve as the cash repository, and makes a sign that reads, "Courtesy of Sue's Bagels! $2 per bagel."

There's nothing left for Sue to do but launch.

Failing Fast: Test, Review, Repeat

Sue still has many unanswered questions. How many bagels should she make per office? Is $2 the right price? How many people will just steal her bagels instead of putting money in the cash box? Should she offer cream cheese and other condiments?

> If you are not embarrassed by the first version of your product, you've launched too late.
>
> —Reid Hoffman (Cofounder and Executive Chairman, LinkedIn)

But even though she has so many questions, Sue also has some hard *facts* on her Business Model Canvas. She knows convenience is the priority, and thanks to her key partnerships, the office managers, she knows exactly how many people work at each office.

As for what she doesn't know, there are some questions that can only be answered by observing customer behavior. And while the Efficiency Roadmap process has certainly eliminated some of the risks in starting a business, it's impossible to remove *all* risk. Ultimately, a small-business owner has to know when she has enough information to take action.

For Sue, that time has come.

So the next day, she wakes up well before dawn and makes more bagels than she's ever made in her life. She boxes them up and loads them into her car. She frantically drives around to each of the ten offices and delivers the bagels as soon as the office managers arrive. Then she goes home, cleans up the mess, and goes back to the offices around lunchtime to collect her cash and strategize for the next day. She'll have to buy more ingredients and decide what kind of experiments she's going to run in order to collect information about her customers' preferences.

On the first day of Sue's official launch, her sales revenue is pretty depressing.

She had made five hundred bagels at a cost of about twenty-five cents each, and then she delivered fifty bagels to each of the ten offices. But she only pulled in about $20 per office. About half the bagels had been eaten, but less than half of the people were paying for them. Her CFO explained that between her Cost of Goods Sold (including electricity to run her oven for all those hours), gas for her car, and the 20 percent cut for the office managers, Sue was on pace to gross about $1,000 per week—but she would only take home about $125 of that. Since most offices are open about forty-seven weeks per year, after accounting for holidays, Sue was on track to make *less than $6,000 a year* working *full-time* at this new job. That was *less than half* of minimum wage! That's what you call a fail.

But Sue is in a "fail fast" mentality now. She never expected to hit a home run in her first week. So she pivots, designs some new tests, and keeps going.

She plays with the quantity of bagels she delivers to each office and the size, wording, and design of her sign. It turns out that the size and placement of the sign matters. The number of pilfered bagels goes down. She also tries offering cream cheese at certain locations with an option that reads "$2 for a plain bagel. $3 for a bagel with cream cheese." Turns out, people love their cream cheese, and they're willing to pay for it. Bagel sales go up, with the majority of them being three-dollar sales instead of two-dollar sales. And when she tries putting out her own cream cheese—homemade and branded with "Sue's Bagels"—sales go even higher.

A few weeks later, as she's driving home one day with all the bagels she didn't sell, Sue has a big idea.

She calls the local food bank.

Then she changes the wording of her signs at some locations to indicate a partnership with Feeding America; some of her proceeds will now help local food-insecure families. The sign now reads, "Suggested donation of $2 per plain bagel or $3 for a bagel with cream cheese." This one's a game changer. All of a sudden, bagel consumption ticks up by about 20 percent, and the amount of money collected goes up by over 40 percent, because almost no one takes a bagel without paying for it. What's more, on average, people are paying *more* than the suggested donation.

Over a couple months in business, Sue's Bagels goes from projected net earnings of $6,000 per year to about $35,000—a nearly six-fold increase. And that number is growing all the time, even after giving 5 percent of net profits to Feeding America.

She's also discovered an entirely new core value proposition.

Through her alliance with Feeding America, Sue transformed a simple transaction—bagels for money—into something bigger. Her

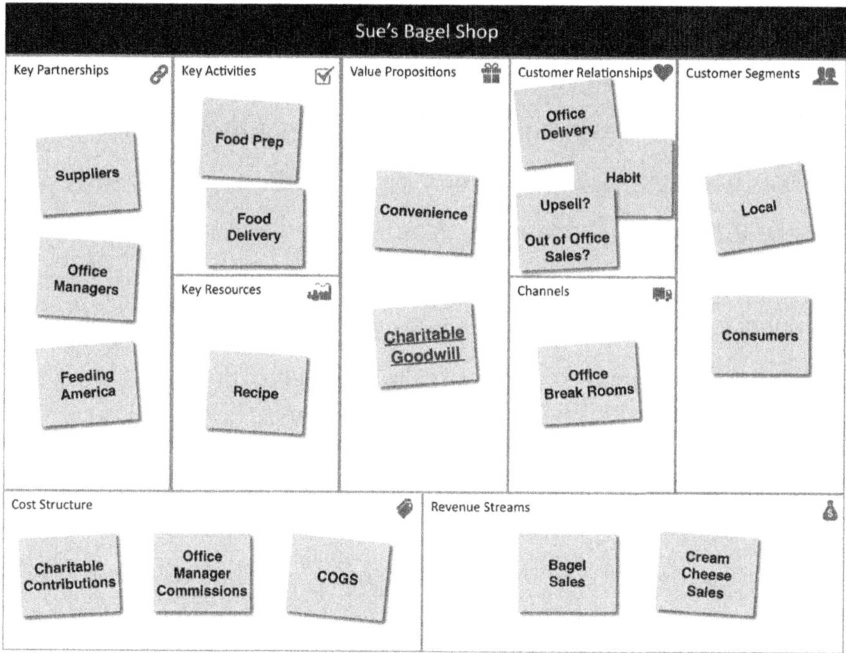

customers now feel that they're making a difference just by buying breakfast. Sue has created a ton of value for them: She's delivering an ultraconvenient (and delicious) breakfast, *and* she's giving them a chance to feel better about themselves. Sue isn't *speculating* that she's creating all this value for her customers; she *knows* she is, because they're stuffing money into her cash box every day.

Sue didn't exactly set out to engage in social entrepreneurship; that is, she didn't plan on building a business that would make money while also alleviating hunger in her local neighborhood. But now that she's sending a check to the local food bank every single week—something that the food-bank director tells her is making a real difference for local families—Sue's business feels a lot more rewarding than she'd ever imagined it would.

Any way you slice it, Sue has herself a business.

The Lifestyle Off-ramp

At the end of the last chapter, when it looked like Sue's chances for success were slim to none, I introduced the idea of the rip cord off-ramp. That's the opportunity to abandon a sinking entrepreneurial ship before drowning yourself and your finances along with it.

Sue is now at the helm of a growing and successful small business, and she's arrived at her first major decision point about the business's direction and her own role in it. That means she has the option of taking a different off-ramp: the *lifestyle* off-ramp.

The lifestyle off-ramp means the small-business owner intentionally controls the size of his business, so that running it is a job he can do largely on his own and on his own terms. Many small-business owners don't *want* to grow their business into an empire; the lifestyle off-ramp is their ultimate dream. Part I of this book showed how the efficiency of passion and the Golden Formula—in which you focus on raising the value of each hour of your time—make DIYing an inefficient way to run a business. Yet for the small-business owners who choose the lifestyle off-ramp and want nothing more than to perform the key activities of their business while earning a living doing it, then that inefficiency can be a conscious choice. For a select few, it's the road to happiness. In fact, when I meet with small-business owners in my work at Agents of Efficiency, I often ask them to rate the efficiency of their business on a one-to-ten scale. The most common answer I get is a three, and some of them are perfectly content with that.

How about Sue? At this point, she can choose to continue making bagels out of her home kitchen and delivering them herself.

She has a nice little business: low budget, relatively easy, and quite rewarding. Though she may be able to add a couple more offices to her customer base, she'll quickly run out of kitchen capacity and hours in the day. But by that point, and by continuing to refine and improve her business model, she'll probably be earning a decent living, and perhaps more than she was making at her old job.

If there's nothing Sue loves more than the smell of bagels baking in her home kitchen while sending a weekly check to Feeding America and having a few minutes every day to shoot the breeze with the office managers who are her key partners, then the lifestyle off-ramp is the perfect choice for her.

Just a few months ago, Sue would have killed to have her own "lifestyle business" that would pay her about the same as she was making before, while also allowing her to be her own boss *and* raise money for charity. But the past few months have been quite a whirlwind and have gotten her to think a little differently. She wonders if there is an even bigger future ahead of her.

She also wonders if baking and delivering bagels day in and day out will get old. Plus, there's one thing about it that scares her: What if another bagel shop—maybe a big one, like Einstein Bros. Bagels—steals her idea and puts her out of business?

That possibility really bothers her. And suddenly, as sure as the entrepreneurial itch that made her take a leap of faith and start her own business in the first place, Sue becomes obsessed with this new worry: *How will she stay ahead of the competition?*

Though she sure never thought of herself as a small-business "visionary," she loved developing her business model. There was all the excitement of coming up with the ideas, testing the hypotheses, failing and then succeeding—and succeeding again. She didn't just *like* being a small-business visionary; she *loved* it. What would be her next idea? How could she build her business into something that the competition could never undermine?

No, the lifestyle off-ramp isn't for Sue. She's on her way to becoming a big-time CEO.

8

Flourish: Live Free

It is the ultimate luxury to combine passion and contribution. It's also a very clear path to happiness.

—Sheryl Sandberg
(COO, Facebook)

Sue had a big realization at the end of the last chapter: She decided the lifestyle off-ramp wasn't for her. She wants to make her business bigger and better and to carve out a place for herself as a CEO.

Up until this point, though, Sue has been DIYing her entire business; currently, the only difference between Sue and "Sue's Bagels" is a name and a legal fiction.

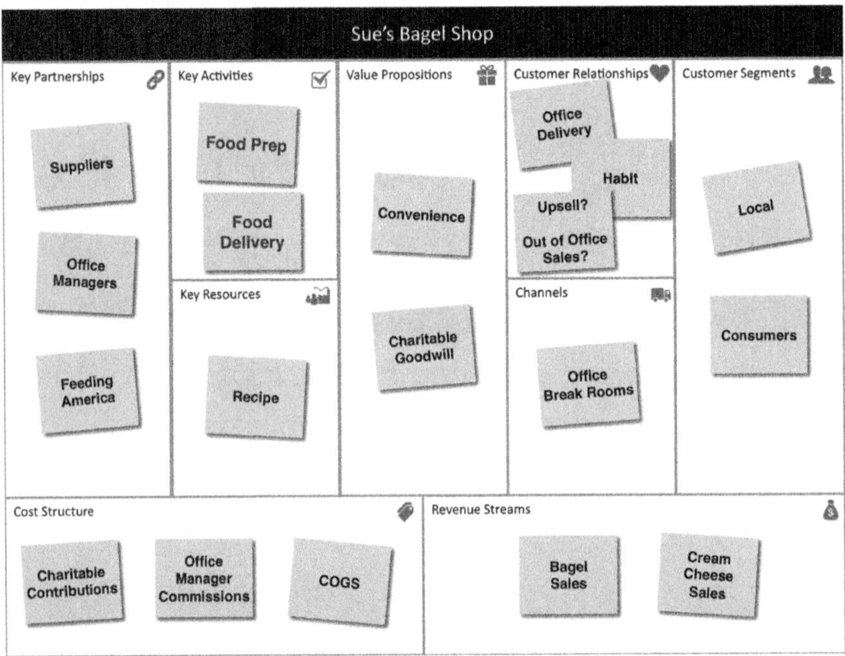

But Sue wants a different path. She wants to make her business something big.

Using the "slow is fast" approach, she's already put herself on strong footing. She tested product-market fit to come up with a great business model. She diligently tested the assumptions behind her value proposition and customer segments. That process led to a big discovery about her distribution channel, and to changing her model from storefront to direct delivery. And once she started delivering to office break rooms, she ran still more experiments: She tested different approaches to her display and the wording on her sign, and soon she game up with the brilliant idea of a partnership with Feeding America.

At this point, and with the exception of a few question marks under "Customer Relationships," the right side of Sue's Business Model Canvas is looking pretty tight.

In fact, up until this point, Sue has directed all her attention to the right side—the *value* side—of her canvas.

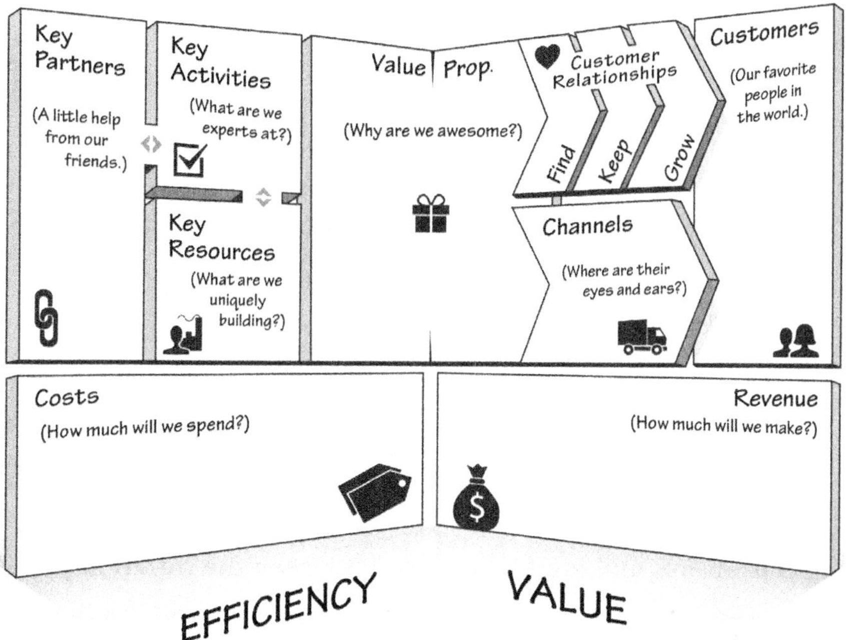

That means Sue hasn't really given much thought at all to the left side—the *efficiency* side—of her Business Model Canvas. But with her value proposition now so clearly defined, and with her decision not to take the lifestyle off-ramp, it's time for Sue to turn her attention to efficiency. She's been focused on the first of our two fundamental questions up until this point, but now she takes a hard look at the second one:

1. CREATE VALUE: How can I create the maximum value possible for my clients?
2. **CREATE EFFICIENCY: How can I capture the maximum share of that value for myself?**

At first, the question seems daunting; she doesn't know how she's going to capture the *maximum* value for herself. But she knows she wants to build a successful business, and that she wants to be the CEO.

The Role of the Owner–CEO

Now that Sue is ready to bring her business to scale, she's got to take a hard look at her own responsibilities. Most CEOs at large companies don't execute any of the key activities of the companies they lead. What do they do instead?

The CEO lives and breathes the Business Model Canvas. The CEO holds that big-picture vision in his head and is constantly looking for ways to improve it, both on the right and the left sides of the canvas, and in how the two sides fit together. A CEO is always looking for "friction" between the different parts of the business model, and for ways to reduce that friction. A CEO takes the long view, yet maintains an obsessive focus on the bottom line.

Sue's impressive work developing a tight product-market fit is certainly consistent with the work of a CEO. At the same time, though, she's been executing all of her business's core activities. If she truly wants to be a CEO, she has to stop doing the key activities. If she tries to do everything—grow the business while still doing everything herself—she'll run out of hours in the day and she'll push herself to the breaking point. And if she gets so busy that she can't take care of her partner and customer relationships, she'll probably compromise her core value proposition too.

Many small-business owners bring themselves and their businesses right up to this breaking point. But **the solution lies in getting out from under those key activities and clearing up a dangerous misunderstanding about compensation and profit.**

Right now, Sue thinks she's already built a profitable business. But she hasn't.

You might disagree. At last count, Sue was pulling in about $35,000 per year net of expenses, and growing fast. But that assessment was ignoring a critical item on Sue's balance sheet: her own salary.

To put it more accurately, Sue doesn't have a profitable business; she has a *job*. And it's primarily *not* the job of a CEO if she itemizes the duties in her job description. Sue's current job pays $35,000 per year for making bagels from her home kitchen, delivering those bagels, and collecting money and uneaten bagels at the end of the day. She's on pace to work about 2,000 hours a year, so at this point, she's created a job for herself that pays about $17.50 hourly with no benefits. If Sue were to do an apples-to-apples comparison to a W-2 employee who is earning the same salary but also getting benefits, her hourly rate would be closer to $12.50.

That's not exactly CEO-level pay, which makes sense because she's not yet doing primarily CEO-level work. But is she getting *any* CEO-level pay? How high (or low) is her $12.50 hourly rate for the type of work she *is* doing?

Remembering the Golden Formula from Chapter Two, Sue asks herself three questions.

1. **Where am I spending my time?**

Currently, Sue is (1) making bagels from her home kitchen, (2) driving all over town delivering those bagels and collecting money for them, (3) managing all the little details of keeping her business afloat, and (4) doing the high-level, business-model-design work of a CEO.

2. **What is the cost of my labor?**

In an apples-to-apples comparison to a job with an employer that includes some limited benefits, Sue is paying herself the market equivalent of $12.50 per hour to do all of these tasks.

But that number doesn't capture the true cost of her labor. Sue was making $42.50 per hour at her day job before she quit to start her bagel shop. That's the fair market value of her time. So for every hour she chooses to invest in her new business instead of going back to work for an employer, it effectively costs her $42.50. Put another way, each hour she works is the equivalent of a $42.50 investment in her business.

3. **How much value am I adding to my business?**

To answer this question, Sue thinks for a few minutes about how much she'd have to pay someone else to do these tasks for her. She could probably pay minimum wage to a driver for delivering the bagels and picking up the locked cash boxes. As for actually making the bagels, that's a bit harder, because Sue hates to admit that someone else could make the bagels as well as she does. But really it's the recipe that matters, and she could train someone else to do the baking. Hiring a baker would probably cost in the neighborhood of $12 to $15 hourly.

And what about the visioning work she's doing in order to build her business from scratch? It's hard to put a precise number on that but she feels certain it's the stuff that commands a six-figure salary.

The Golden Formula has revealed a couple important truths to Sue. For starters, she realizes that her business is *not* profitable. Not yet, anyway.

Question: How do you know when your business is profitable?

Answer: You have a profitable business when you can cover all relevant expenses *and* pay a market-rate salary to *someone else* for performing the business's key activities, *and* still have money left over.

In Sue's case, her business would be profitable only if $35,000 could cover all labor and expenses and pull in some money on top of that. But she knows it would cost more than $35,000 a year to pay competent people fair market rates to do all the jobs she's doing herself. That means her business only *looks* profitable right now because she's doing some work at below-market rates in order to keep the business afloat.

Indeed, Sue now realizes that there's a $30-per-hour difference between her fair market wage and the rate she's actually paying herself. Each hour she works on her business is the equivalent of a $42.50 investment; if she then draws $12.50 in wages, she's investing $30 in her business for every hour she works.

That isn't necessarily a bad thing. Every business requires investment—in time, money, and talent. From the start, Sue has been willing to invest herself and all her available resources in her business, and it's an investment she hopes will yield a big return at some point down the road.

At the same time, as you read back in Chapter Two, successful business owners are always seeking to increase their effective hourly rate. And Sue realizes it's time for her to think about increasing her own hourly rate—not by drawing more in wages, but by increasing the value she creates in each hour she works. She knows that's the path to profitability.

And currently, she's using half her time to be a bagel chauffeur, so it's no wonder she's only taking home $12.50 per hour.

She's got to hire someone else.

Of course, hiring a new employee is always easier said than done. After all, Sue's only pulling in $35,000 per year. Where's this extra money going to come from?

The Path to Profitability

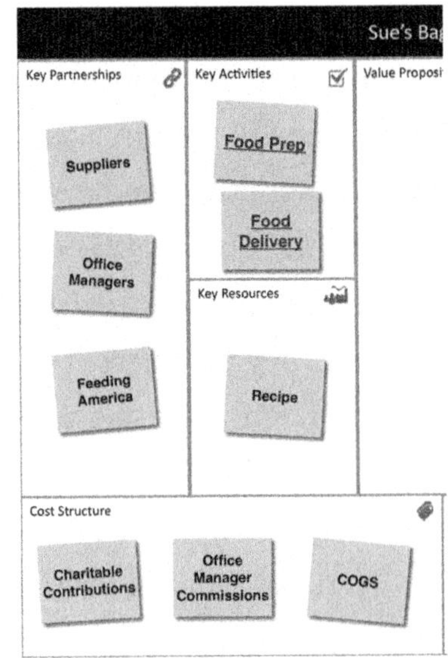

For Sue, as for most small-business owners, her path to profitability starts with changing her relationship to the Key Activities section of her Business Model Canvas. What's more, her COO has told her that the way out of the DIY trap is usually through either Key Partnerships or Key Resources. And given the success of her partnership with office managers, she briefly considers whether or not something like Uber could be her best bet for executing the bagel-chauffeuring activity. Eventually, she decides against it, though, and determines that hiring a regular employee is the way to go.

Now for the question of how to pay this person. One answer would be to get a part-time job. Instead of investing all of her $42.50-per-hour time in her business, she could go back to work for her former employer a few hours a week and then use her earnings to hire a driver. But Sue decides that isn't what she wants to do. (Still, this is an important reason not to lose sight of your fair market wage; you need that number to properly assess all available options when you need capital for your business.)

Sue has never lost sight of the fact that she was going to put herself into about $400,000 of debt by pursuing a storefront for her bagel business. That level of financial investment was a risk she was ready and willing to take. When she refined her value proposition to the office break room concept, however, she came up with a business model that required no debt at all. But she sees now that zero debt might be a little unrealistic, and she reaches a conclusion that many small-business owners come to at some point in time.

The most common source of capital for small-business owners isn't a check from the bank, and it certainly isn't a bigger check from a venture capitalist. It's the unsexy and often painful process of sacrificing personal compensation. It's a short-term decision made with an eye toward a bigger future—but it's no less uncomfortable because of it.

Rather than paying themselves every penny the company can afford, many small-business owners cut their own compensation to use that money for growing the business, with the hope of earning a much bigger salary down the road. Sue is willing to take this long view. She's going to use that $35,000 to grow her business instead of paying herself. And she decides not to seek part-time work to earn money; it's a big sacrifice, but it's one she wants to make.

So Sue hires a driver, and immediately, her workload is cut in half. By the time she factors in payroll taxes, benefits, and all the costs of bringing this minimum-wage employee on board to work about one thousand hours per year for her, Sue's projected take-home compensation has dropped by about $10,000, from $35,000 to $25,000 per year. But her own market-equivalent hourly rate just rose from $12.50 per hour to $17.50 per hour, because she's no longer performing minimum-wage work herself. And that math includes a fourth addition to Sue's C-suite: She brings in a CHRO. At a very modest cost, she's hired a Professional Employer Organization (PEO) to handle all HR responsibilities. That decision brings along the side benefit of, well, benefits. The PEO sets up her business with a 401(k) and health insurance. Sue will be able to enroll herself in those benefits when the time is right—though she decides she's not quite there yet, because she still wants to use all available cash to invest in the business.

And what's her next investment? Well, by hiring a driver, Sue has freed up one thousand hours of time in her own schedule. It's time she could spend earning about $42,500 at a part-time job, netting her $32,500 per year—an immediate 325 percent annual ROI on her investment in a driver. But that's *not* Sue's plan. When it comes to Sue's take-home pay, she's mapping out a strategy in years, not months.

So Sue's next investment is to use that extra one thousand hours of time to *really* start growing the business. When she was doing everything herself, she only had time to deliver to ten or so break rooms, but now she sets about doubling that number.

And just like that, she does it.

Pretty soon, she's employing *two* drivers who are working a *combined* two thousand hours per year. She's bringing in a lot more money too; she now has about $50,000 left over after all expenses, including paying both drivers and making contributions to Feeding America, to use however she wants.

In the meantime, though, Sue is still doing all the baking herself. And at an effective hourly rate of $17.50, she's way overpaid as a baker—and still way underpaid in terms of the fair market value of her time if she were to work elsewhere. She sits down with her Business Model Canvas and looks at Key Activities. There it is: Food Prep.

But freeing herself from baking is more complicated than simply hiring a driver to deliver bagels. Part of the reason, she realizes, is that she's been ignoring an important resource in her business model: her kitchen.

The Hazard—and Opportunity—of Hidden Resources

Sue had never thought of putting her home kitchen under Key Resources on her Business Model Canvas. Now she realizes that if she'd been paying fair-market rent for a kitchen all along, her business would be deep in the red.

Her situation isn't unusual. **Small businesses abound with hidden resources and those hidden resources can often act as choke points to growth.** Sue has been taking her kitchen for granted all this time, and now that she's ready to grow, she doesn't see how she can do it on her shoestring budget. Thanks to her early research into renting a storefront, she knows exactly how expensive an industrial kitchen would be, and on top of that, she was planning to hire a baker. How can she possibly do all that? She finds herself staring dismally at her Business Model Canvas.

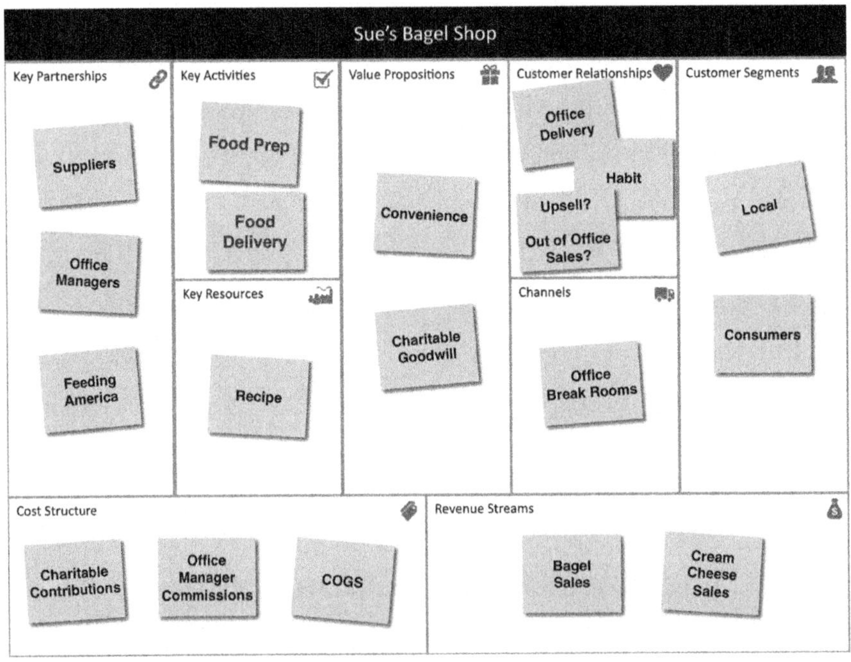

Her eyes are drawn to the sticky note at the very center of her canvas. Convenience is her core value proposition, and the bedrock of her business model.

For a moment, that makes Sue feel even worse because she knows shelling out big bucks for an industrial kitchen won't enhance that value proposition one bit. Her customers don't care where the bagels are made. A new kitchen would overburden her

Cost Structure while adding zero value for her customers, and she has been at this long enough to know that's a bad formula.

She also feels dumb for never having put her home kitchen under Key Resources. In fact, her family's bagel recipe is the only thing she ever listed as an important resource.

And that gets her thinking about whether the recipe is really a core ingredient to her company's success. She knows it's not quality, but rather, convenience that her customers really care about.

It's hard for her to admit it. It's so dramatically different from her first vision of Sue's Bagels. But the recipe isn't what matters at all. She rips the "Recipe" sticky note from her canvas.

And then, as she looks at the empty box for Key Resources, she has the idea that liberates her from the weight of performing Key Activities *and* from the trap of hidden resources.

Sue needs a co-packer!

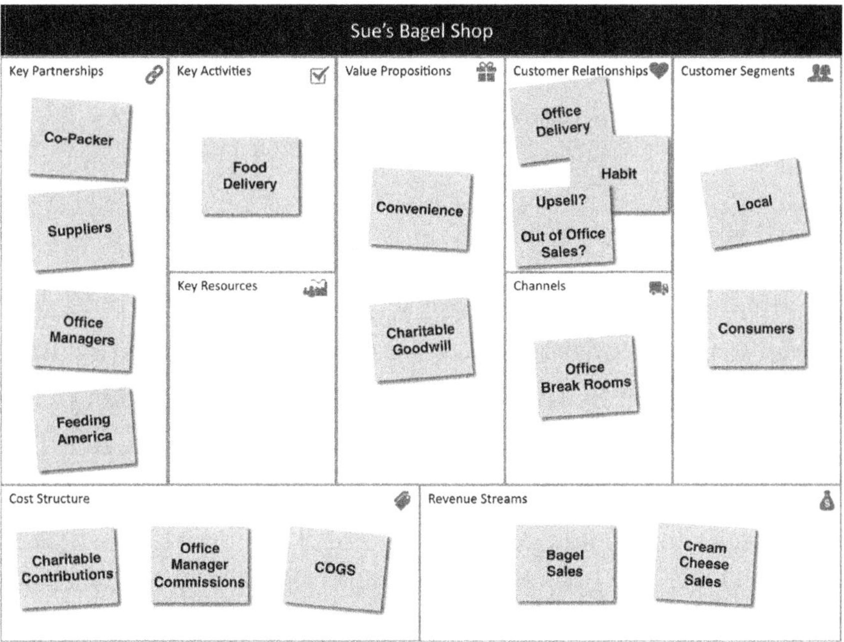

It makes sense. Sue's partnership with office managers was the game-changer that converted her bagel idea from certain failure into a sustainable business. And now, a new partnership—with a co-packer— would clear the way for explosive growth.

After talking the idea over with her COO, Sue sets to work doing the considerable research necessary to identify the right co-packer to meet her needs. She finds the perfect one. It's located in the Bronx and specializes in bagels. And as much as she hates to admit it, she knows this might even raise the quality of her product—because New York water is one of the reasons New York bagels are the best. Not to mention the impressive fact that this co-packer supplies bagels to the likes of Starbucks and the Waldorf Astoria. Sue figures, if their bagels are tasty enough for the Waldorf Astoria, her customers in office break rooms are going to be quite happy.

With the help of her CFO, Sue turns to the numbers.

Bringing in a co-packer is going to increase her cost of goods sold by *a lot*. Each bagel will now cost Sue seventy-five cents, whereas she had estimated that each bagel cost her about twenty-five cents when she was making them herself. But in talking this over with her CFO, Sue realizes that she had left some important things out of that estimate of twenty-five cents.

She'd been taking her home kitchen for granted, both as a resource and in terms of the wear and tear she was causing by using it for commercial baking. If she had factored in those things, she would have come up with a number much higher than twenty-five cents. But what's more, that twenty-five-cent figure made absolutely no attempt to account for the value of Sue's time as the baker. Suddenly, the co-packer doesn't seem so expensive, especially when compared with renting a commercial kitchen and hiring a baker.

There's still an immediate hit to Sue's bottom line, though. At last count, Sue had about $50,000 in annual revenue to invest back into her business. The addition of a co-packer would eat up nearly all of that; it was going to cost her $47,000. She'd have a measly $3,000 remaining.

It was a big move, and one Sue wouldn't be able to afford if she hadn't temporarily cut her own salary. But she knows it is the right way forward—not only to liberate her from baking, but to position her company for robust growth in the future.

In fact, because of the co-packer's price structure, this transition will save Sue far more money down the line. The more bagels Sue orders from the co-packer, the lower the unit cost. That is, if Sue doubles the size of her order, the per-bagel price of seventy-five cents would drop substantially. In terms of her bottom line, **future growth in the business will bring not only more revenue, but also a greater profit margin on each sale. *That's* a recipe for long-term success**. What's more, Sue knows her business is about to enter a phase of unfettered growth because she has now freed up her own time to focus on that very thing.

Leveraging Hidden Resources to Your Competitive Advantage

Uncovering hidden resources is the key to survival for many businesses, whether at the stage of start-up, exponential growth, or a pivot in a changing marketplace.

As an example, I recently worked with a video production company in need of a pivot in their business model. Their revenue was shrinking and, at the same time, they had a large office complex weighing down their balance sheet. The solution: Turn that liability into an asset. They carved up their office space and furnished it to be a co-working space that other entrepreneurs and small businesses could rent on the cheap, but they kept their green screen and all their video production equipment as a value-add for their tenants—one that made them stand out from the co-working space competition.

What are the hidden resources in your business?

Unfettered Growth

What is Sue's first order of business now that she's freed up her time and can truly focus on growing the business?

She goes back to her Business Model Canvas. She figures she might as well start by filling in the gaps since, right now, her canvas

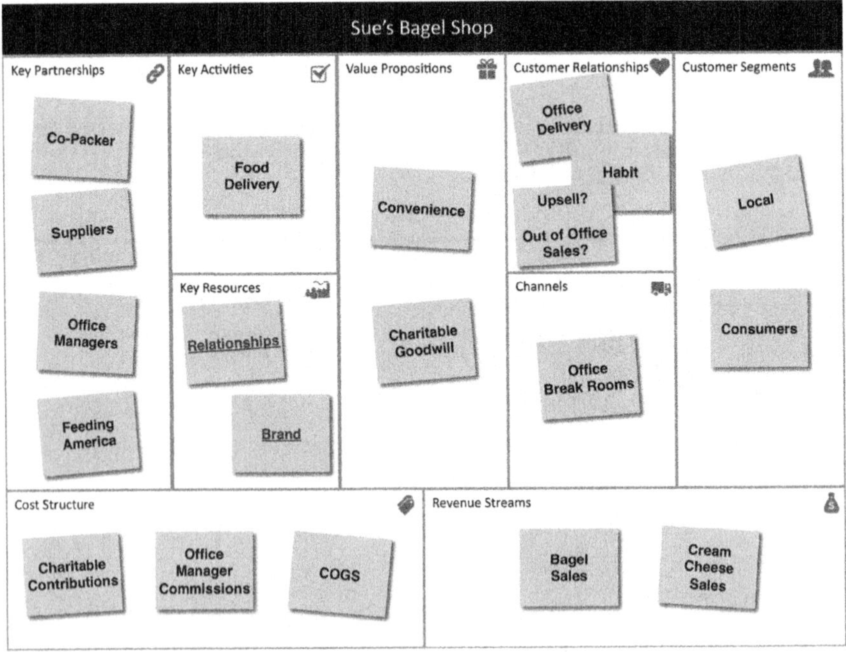

shows *zero* Key Resources. She knows that's not true; of course she has important resources, or she wouldn't have been able to come so far so fast. But what are they?

Then, looking at the words "Charitable Goodwill" under Value Proposition, the answer hits her: relationships!

Sue has already established some important relationships with office managers as well as with the local food-bank director through Feeding America. *Of course* relationships are a key resource!

Relationships are *also* the answer to the question that's been in the back of Sue's mind ever since she decided between the lifestyle off-ramp and the life of a CEO: How will Sue prevent a competitor—especially a much larger competitor—from stealing her idea and wiping out her business?

The answer is *relationships*, and eventually, with the power of her brand. Currently, office break rooms are a wide-open field; there was no company that had made its name synonymous with break-room breakfast the way Coke, for example, was synonymous with cola. Sue is claiming that space for herself. And she could use strong relationships—and the powerful goodwill she'd created through her alliance with Feeding America—to quickly establish a trusted brand name. Once in place, that brand would be difficult for even a large corporation to disrupt, just the way Apple and Google can't unseat Dropbox.

Sue is starting to see a clear path to turning her tiny enterprise into a successful—and *national*—company. But achieving that kind of scale would require a few more tweaks to her Business Model Canvas.

If she really went national, she wouldn't be able to meet one-on-one with every office manager. That seemed to run counter to the idea that relationships were one of her two Key Resources. But maybe not?

Maybe she just needs to think a little bigger, in terms of which relationships she is focused on building, and whether she thinks of them as partners or customers. She looks at the sticky that reads "Office Managers," and pulls it off her canvas. On a fresh sticky note, she writes "Office-Complex Management Companies," and then, instead of placing it under Key Partnerships, she puts it under Customer Segments.

After all, Sue's product didn't just create value for the individual consumers who ate the bagels. Entire offices now enjoyed free breakfast delivery and had the good feeling of participating in a program that helped to feed local food-insecure families. And, all else being equal, if you were looking to rent office space for your company, which office complex would you chose: the one that included breakfast delivery or the one that didn't?

Sue had started out offering the office managers a 20 percent cut of her proceeds, but she sees now that she might be able to eliminate that expense. If she thought of office-complex management companies as one of her customer segments—and if she did some research and hypothesis-testing to better understand their needs—she thinks she just might be able to make a strong value proposition that doesn't involve giving them a 20 percent cut. They would get some great marketing credit for bringing in a company allied with Feeding America, plus, she would add the considerable value of providing free breakfast-delivery service to their tenants. If Sue could eliminate the office managers' 20 percent cut from her cost structure, her profit margin would skyrocket.

Sue is downright giddy. She pulls the sticky note that reads "Local" from the Customer Segments area of her canvas, and throws it in the trash.

Then she laughs. At the top of her canvas it still says "Sue's Bagel Shop." Her business definitely isn't a shop—and really, it isn't necessarily bagels, either. It is convenience and charitable goodwill, in the form of breakfast delivery.

"I guess I shouldn't limit myself to bagels," she says out loud, remembering some of her first customer interviews, in which pretty much everyone said they occasionally grabbed a donut or a Danish in place of a bagel, depending on their mood.

Maybe providing a mix of breakfast pastries would make her business even greater, the way adding cream cheese in her first week had caused sales to spike. She knows she can find another co-packer as easily as she'd found the first. She makes yet another change to her Business Model Canvas.

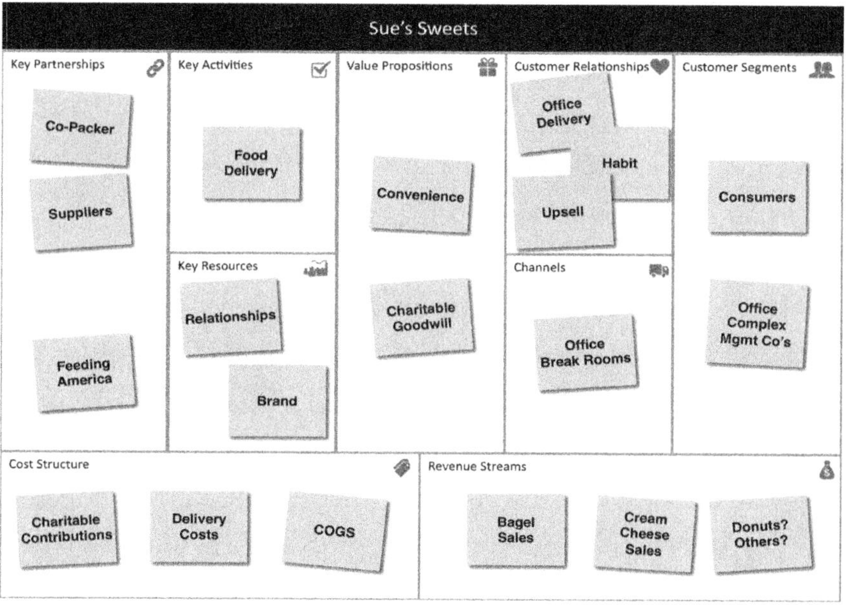

Sue's business model has now come a long way from her initial idea: that storefront at 123 Main Street. She sure hadn't set out to build a nationwide office-food-delivery empire. But her bagel shop business model was full of unpleasant surprises that would have left her doomed for failure. Meanwhile, her new model has yielded a whole bunch of *pleasant* surprises, and she is loving every minute of being a CEO.

The Ultimate Off-ramp

Sue isn't done, of course. Soon, she'll hire a few more staff members, then *lots* of staff members, as quickly as she can bring them on. She'll focus on building relationships with office-complex management companies, and deepen her relationship with Feeding America. Soon, she'll need to bring in the final member of her small-business C-suite—her CMO—to build out a sales team to take herself out of that process. For each of these steps, process will be key. She will constantly look for ways to improve the efficiency of her business. She will continuously evaluate how much value her employees create for her customer segments, because the first hint of wasted time is an opportunity for a competitor to swoop in.

At some point, Sue will evaluate her own role as CEO. Once she brings on a CMO, Sue herself will no longer be responsible for growing the customer base, and there may not be a lot for her to do. She will have made herself obsolete—the surest sign she's built herself a business. At that point, she'll be able to retire if she wants to, and sit back while the money rolls in. Maybe she'll want to stay on as founder and chair of the board. Maybe by that point, she'll want to just spend time with her family, or travel, or perhaps start a nonprofit. Or maybe she'll have an idea for a whole new direction for Sue's Sweets, and she'll pour all her energy into pursuing that new vision and unlocking those new opportunities for growth. No matter what she decides, she has reached the ultimate goal; she's at the ultimate off-ramp, with complete freedom to choose her next path.

Sue's Sweets will still face challenges ahead, of course, whether or not Sue herself is there to manage them. Like every business operating in the twenty-first century, her business will face the Digital Revolution. In particular, **in a world where technology improves on a daily basis, how can a small business keep up? What does it mean to be truly efficient in the Digital Age? The answers matter for *your* business. That's ahead.**

PART III

AUTOMATE THE BORING STUFF, BECAUSE PASSION PRODUCES PROFIT

We're in the midst of industrial change every bit as powerful as the First Industrial Revolution. The Digital Revolution is changing everything; it's killing whole industries, and creating new ones. That change is here to stay. Some businesses will ride the wave, while others will drown in it. And that's why this section introduces specific tools and tactics to help you flourish while the competition flails.

In this section you'll find:

1. Why the Digital Revolution is your friend and *not* your enemy.
2. How to use technology to increase the value you deliver to your customers *and* the profit you take home.
3. How cutting-edge technology has paved the way for you to build a smarter workforce that operates more efficiently at a lower cost, with better results for you *and* your staff.
4. Why small is big in the Digital Age, and how you can outcompete huge competitors by leveraging your unique assets.

9

The Digital Revolution: Like it or not, you can't ignore it. Ride the wave or drown in it.

Fluctuat Nec Mergitur

"He who rises with the wave is not swallowed by it."

—The Official Motto of the City of Paris

You might not think your small business has anything in common with the craft textile weavers of late eighteenth-century England.

When the Industrial Revolution swept through Britain and Europe, there were winners and losers. Mechanized textile production made some people filthy rich, as wealthy entrepreneurs erected the first modern factories and churned out goods for a global market. As a result, much of the general populace enjoyed a sustained increase in its standard of living, since quality goods were now available on the cheap. Meanwhile, abysmal working conditions hurt many; labor laws eventually came on the books to protect them. And master textile weavers found themselves out of work, as their handmade products became obsolete.

That was the First Industrial Revolution. Then there was the Second Industrial Revolution, in the twentieth century, when Henry Ford developed the factory assembly line. And now there's a *third* industrial revolution afoot: the Digital Revolution.

The advent of the factory in the eighteenth century forever changed the production of goods, from bespoke craftsmanship to mechanical process, and dramatically reduced costs for the end consumer. The second revolution brought the dawn of mass production, and once again changed the way goods were produced and the cost to obtain them. Now the Digital Revolution is applying the concepts of mechanization, automation, and mass production not to goods but to services—and it's effecting a fundamental change in the way services are delivered in the twenty-first century.

Following are just a few examples.

Traditional stockbrokers have lost market share to websites like E*TRADE, and to robo-advisors like Betterment. Banks are allowing customers to deposit checks via ATMs and mobile apps, reducing the need for human bank tellers. And with the growing acceptance of the block-chain system first brought into prominence by Bitcoin, it's possible that there will be far more dramatic changes in the banking industry in the not-too-distant future.

Software like TurboTax has done big damage to the traditional accounting industry, and these types of software programs are getting more powerful all the time.

Monster.com and LinkedIn have replaced many professional recruiters.

Receptionists and phone operators are becoming obsolete, since mobile apps and automated telephone systems can perform the same work.

The television industry is changing by the day. Netflix and Hulu have moved much of the TV-watching experience to the computer (or tablet, or smartphone) screen. Many households—especially in the millennial generation—reject cable subscriptions entirely.

A number of travel websites—Travelocity, Expedia, and Priceline, to name a few—have nearly eliminated the demand for old-fashioned human travel agents. Meanwhile Uber, Lyft, and other car-sharing services are taking business from traditional taxi and livery companies. Airbnb and HomeAway are doing the same in the hotel and motel industries.

Those are only a few examples. The digital wave is changing just about everything—and that raises a very important question.

Will You Ride the Wave or Drown in It?

On the one hand, it sounds grim to hear all this talk of master weavers and kindly travel agents and skilled taxi drivers all losing their jobs in a tidal wave of industrial change. But just as the First Industrial Revolution ushered in the beginning of sustained economic growth, and just as the assembly line made the previously unaffordable automobile newly obtainable for middle-class Americans, the Digital Revolution is bringing profound benefits. Powerful technology has found its way to nearly every corner of the earth. Standards of living have improved in countless ways, as laborious or impracticable tasks have become not only possible, but nearly free. If you ask someone whether they'd prefer to be wealthy a hundred years ago or middle-class today, most people will choose the latter because few of us want to give up our smartphone or our toilet.

Meanwhile, in all this change, some people have become very, very wealthy by capitalizing on revolutionary technology to deliver new and better products on an ever-quicker and more affordable scale.

Adapt or Perish

When the automobile industry began to flourish at the end of the nineteenth century, it was a bad time to be in the horse-drawn carriage business, and many carriage manufacturers did not survive long into the twentieth century.[15]

But one company saw an opportunity to use its existing expertise in metalwork for building cars instead. Studebaker Brothers went from carriage manufacturing to a successful automobile business, and actually survived all the way to the 1960s, when it couldn't compete with the scale of manufacturing in Detroit.

And what about you? As a small-business owner at a time of rapid industrial change, you should be asking yourself: *Which side of history am I on?*

I know plenty of accountants who badmouth TurboTax. I know a million lawyers who have no end of bad things to say about Rocket Lawyer and LegalZoom. Taxi drivers malign Uber all day long. And master textile weavers in eighteenth-century England probably weren't huge fans of the cotton mill, either.

So call it a moment of truth. Take a deep breath. And be honest.

Are you resisting change? Are you set on sticking to your old ways?

Or do you want to adapt? Are you ready to seize cutting-edge tools and ever-improving technology, not only to survive, but also to thrive?

Why Lawyers Are Scared S***less and How the Smart Will Succeed

In Chapter One you read about the typical overworked solopreneur lawyer who set up his own law firm and ended up drowning in DIY. In Chapter Three you read about an attorney named Jim, and how building a team of outsourced experts turned his practice from run-of-the-mill (or worse) into a runaway success, because all of a sudden, he had the time and resources to deliver the best legal counsel in his niche.

But thanks to the digital wave, Jim still has more work to do to put his firm among the elite that will thrive in our new era of technology.

Think about it this way. The classic lawyer is a sort of craftsman. Historically, he's considered his *core* duties to include *all* of the following:

- Advocacy: Representing and advocating for clients in courts and negotiations
- Content Creation: Drafting wills, contracts, and pleadings
- Counseling: Providing legal advice
- Process: Helping clients navigate the complex legal system.

And maybe it used to make sense for all of the above to be absolutely essential tasks performed by a skilled lawyer, but then technology arrived and changed everything.

Now lawyers are scared. In fact, their profession more and more looks like the quaint craft of custom tailoring. It used to be that if you needed a suit you went to a tailor. He took your measurements, you discussed design and fabrics, and then, at a cost of thousands of dollars, you'd have yourself a fine suit. These days, very few people buy suits that way, because you can get a pretty good suit off the rack for a fraction of the cost, and then you only need a tailor to make a few adjustments.

It's similar in the legal profession. Let's say you need a lawyer because you're founding your own corporation. A lawyer can draft custom articles of incorporation at a cost of thousands of dollars, just like a tailor can make a suit.

But now sites like Legal Zoom and Rocket Lawyer provide the resources to handle all that—at huge savings for the consumer. Those websites sprung up because the old system was outdated; much of the work traditionally performed by a lawyer can be automated, and some if it can be done by non-lawyer professionals at a very low cost. That's why you can now get your articles of incorporation for a couple hundred bucks, instead of thousands.

Plenty of lawyers are still doing the same work the same way they always have, though. Those lawyers are relying in part on the fact that their clients have never heard of Rocket Lawyer or Legal Zoom. But relying on the ignorance of your client base is not a great business model.

So what's a lawyer to do?

Despite that grim outlook, there's some good news: **Lawyers—and small-business owners, generally—who see the writing on the wall and adapt accordingly have an opportunity to make more money, serve more customers, and have a far more rewarding business than would have been possible in "the good old days."**

And the way to do so is by asking the same questions introduced in Chapter One:

- Where am I spending my time?
- What is the cost of my labor?
- **How much value am I adding to my business?**

The lawyer who's still writing articles of incorporation like a bespoke tailor is spending his time on what he considers core legal practice, and he's probably being paid handsomely for it (for now, at least), but he's not adding value to his business. He's ignoring the profound forces transforming his profession and remaining wedded to an outdated business model. So he's not just failing to *add* value to his firm; he's allowing its value to erode. Eventually, his clients will catch on and he'll be out of a job—not unlike those master weavers in the eighteenth century.

But this is the way he's *always* practiced law; what else is he supposed to do?

For starters, he's approaching the problem from the wrong angle. He's focused on his job description, instead of how to serve his clients. Remember the questions introduced in Chapter Five:

- **CREATE VALUE: How can I create the maximum value possible for my clients?**
- **CREATE EFFICIENCY: How can I capture the maximum share of that value for myself?**

These questions redirect the lawyer's focus to exactly where it should be: how to add value to his customers (rather than relying on their ignorance!); and how to build a truly sustainable business model based on that customer-driven value proposition. In other words, the lawyer has to shift his thinking to focus on his customer. How can he deliver legal services in a way that his clients will value, even as technology continues to advance?

Answer: **Thriving in the Digital Age means putting technology to work on your behalf. If your small business is going to succeed in the Digital Revolution, you've got to utilize every tool available to you in order to increase the value of the work you're doing.**

But how's that possible, you ask, when digital tools are replacing humans all the time?

Well, let's go back to Jim, the attorney from Chapter Three. Let's say that, with help from his trusty COO, Jim retools his practice for the Digital Age. He starts by forswearing any work that can be done cheaply by Rocket Lawyer, and focuses instead on offering expert legal strategy on a client-by-client basis, and delivering it as efficiently as possible while utilizing every relevant digital tool. If a client comes to him for help forming her own corporation, Jim spends as little as fifteen minutes talking with her about her needs, and then he actually *recommends* a service like Legal Zoom for drafting articles of incorporation based on the corporate formation strategy they've just agreed upon.

Or, let's say he has a client with more complex needs who needs something really unique. Once again, he'll have a brief consultation—an hour or less—and then he'll pull in a team of vetted and relatively low-cost lawyers to draft the necessary legal documents. Depending on the complexity of the project, he might even bring in a legal-process outsourcer. But he *doesn't* do that work himself; he focuses his own time on providing expert counsel, and then he meets his clients' subsequent needs by outsourcing.

How do his clients like this twenty-first-century approach to lawyering?

Actually, they *love* it. They pay a fraction of the cost another lawyer would charge, and they still get the expertise, service, and legal documents that they need.

And that's the case even though Jim charges top dollar for his time, the same or even *more* than those high-priced attorneys! The clients don't mind, though, because each one ends up paying for only an hour or less. Yet Jim is now making more money than ever before, because he's using *all* of his time on top-dollar work, and sending the other tasks down the food chain.

Of course, Jim's law office and the legal field generally are just one arena in which technology is changing the way services are valued and delivered. **But whatever your business, technology matters.**

As another example, consider accountants. Software like TurboTax means a lot of the old bread-and-butter accounting work has disappeared. There are plenty of CPAs who've responded by telling everyone who will listen that TurboTax and H&R Block are rubbish, but the trend line suggests otherwise. And as long as these old-fashioned accountants continue to be merely tax technicians, their value is diminishing by the year. Soon, they'll either be working for a fraction of what they used to make or they'll be out of business entirely.

Meanwhile, the savvy accountants are leveraging technology as part of their toolkit and reframing their business model in ways that add more value to their customers. These forward-thinking CPAs realize that a host of low-cost outsourced services—like payroll and bookkeeping outfits, and even speedy tax calculators like TurboTax—could actually be *assets* to them. They see the potential to harness such advances in order to serve their clients in bigger and better ways.

By rethinking their value proposition in ways that add more value to their customers—and by using digital trends to their advantage, instead of fighting them—they're carving out a powerful place for themselves in our new digital world.

They're also developing stronger relationships with their customers by being honest about technology. When you're forthright about the way the Digital Age is changing your industry, your customers will trust you more. Call it karma or whatever you like, but you'll build resilient trust capital with your client base if you're honest about the low-cost digital options available to them. And why *wouldn't* you be honest? You have nothing to fear—because you're building a business model that harnesses those digital tools as one element of a greater product.

Now, **how can you apply all of this to *your specific business*? Ask yourself the following:**

- **Which areas of my business could be done faster and cheaper with digital technology?**
- **In which areas of my business could digital tools help me deliver a better, more valuable product to my customer?**
- **And finally, which are the high-value areas of my business that should never be automated or outsourced?**

By answering these questions honestly, pivoting as necessary, and harnessing cutting-edge tools, you'll build your business model atop the solid bedrock of high-value work. You'll deliver a superior product, serve more clients, and command a higher hourly rate than ever before. And *that's* thriving in the Digital Age.

The Future Is Bright . . . for Some . . .

I talk to small-business owners all the time who are scared of the rapid pace of technological change.

And it *is* scary. It *is* uncertain.

But *your* business is well on its way to thriving in this Third Industrial Revolution because you wouldn't be reading this if you weren't committed to seizing opportunity and making your business as great as it can be.

For that reason, **the next chapter is precisely what you need. It's got the top tech trends that will help your business operate smoother, faster, on a bigger scale, and with a greater profit margin.**

10

Man and Machine: Seven Emerging Tech Trends so Cool You'll Wish They Happened Ten Years Ago

Any sufficiently advanced technology is indistinguishable from magic.

—Arthur C. Clarke
(British Writer, 1917–2008)

Less than a decade ago you would have shelled out the better part of a hundred grand for the kind of business technology that's now available for pennies. On the one hand, that's nothing less than astonishing. On the other hand, it's not unlike the change ushered in by the First Industrial Revolution. Before the advent of the factory, master weavers made textiles by hand and only the wealthy could afford them. Then all of a sudden, just about *everyone* could get ahold of quality fabric. The Industrial Revolution changed everything by automating what had previously been done by hand.

And that's precisely what's ahead in this chapter: cutting-edge tools for your business so that you (and your C-suite, and staff, and outsourcers, and so on) aren't wasting time and money doing stuff that can be done more efficiently by a machine.

Because man *plus* machine wins every time. Whether competing against a machine or a man (or woman) acting alone, the combination of human mind plus machine technology is the winning formula. That was famously evidenced in the sexy world of international chess. Deep Blue, IBM's artificially intelligent chess-playing machine, succeeded at defeating reigning world champion Garry Kasparov. But Kasparov *plus* a machine algorithm could beat Deep Blue—or any human—any day of the week. In chess and in business, technology is essential for playing your best game.

Of course, all of this talk would have been irrelevant a decade ago, when cutting-edge technology was way beyond the price range of a typical small business. It used to be that if you wanted all the power and functionality of Microsoft Exchange and a SharePoint server, you'd have to throw down $10,000 or more just to have the dedicated server in your office. Then you'd have to throw in as much as $50,000 for all the relevant licenses to install the Exchange software, not to mention that you'd then need to hire an IT person to make it all work. Clearly, most small business owners wouldn't even consider forking over that kind of cash. Instead, they'd find other ways to get their e-mail.

But today? You can get Office 365 e-mail for five bucks a month, and you can get the full Office 365 suite with all the software and unlimited downloads for another twenty. Computing power that used to be available only to the largest corporations is now available to even the teeniest start-up.

It gets better. It's not just that the best technology is no longer confined to big business; it's that big business now regularly falls *behind* small businesses and individual consumers.

This is the phenomenon that's been called the *consumerization* of technology. Pretty much up until 2007, technology was geared toward the business sector, because that's who could afford it. Then Steve Jobs announced the iPhone, and coders around the world rushed to develop apps for that new platform. In short order, the best technology and the newest, hottest apps were now available for a couple hundred dollars. Today, workers at the base of many large corporate pyramids come into the office carrying iPads, and they're asking their IT people why a free app is easier to use and more effective than a system the company spent fifty grand to implement five years earlier.

That's a powerful change in a few years.

But think back just a little further, to the 1980s and early 1990s. Computers were just arriving on the scene. And what did everyone say? They said these machines were going to make everyone's job obsolete. They were envisioning a doomsday in which computers did everything, and everyone was unemployed and impoverished.

Not quite how it worked out.

Computers did bring a big change, though: People became more productive. A *lot* more productive. There's no better example of this than the shipping industry. Remember back in Chapter One when I talked about the strange world of international shipping? When I first learned how to create stowage plans for container ships, we used sheets of eleven-by-seventeen paper. Literally, I took colored pencils and filled in the little squares to indicate which cargo should go where. Then I had to use a calculator to manually compute the ship's stability and trip. If that sounds tedious and painful, it was. And then, once the plan was finished, it had to be physically delivered to the ship. So you had to live next door to the terminal, or pretty darn close. Meanwhile, mistakes were inevitable; when you're doing things with colored pencils and a calculator, mistakes happen. And those mistakes had amazingly expensive consequences on the ship.

How do port captains do that same work in 2016? Well, it takes about thirty minutes to do what used to take twelve hours, and instead of being tedious, it's more like a computer game. It still requires intellectual energy, because you've got to get it right. But no longer do they waste any of that energy and precious (expensive) time on monotonous markings and calculations. And once the plan is finished, they just e-mail it off and it arrives instantly. So the job of designing stowage plans didn't disappear with the advent of computer software, but it takes a fraction of the time, and the product is better every time.

And even this process may look slow, inefficient, and antiquated in just a few more years, when still newer and better technology emerges. That's why, whether you're in shipping or any other industry, you've got to view technology as your friend, not your enemy. **The only way technology becomes your enemy is if you close your eyes and pretend it doesn't exist.** Imagine a shipping company trying to compete in today's market while still using eleven-by-seventeen sheets of paper to create stowage plans. That old-school competitor might complain that technology is making them obsolete. But technology isn't their problem. It's their unwillingness to adopt new tools to do what they've always done, only a whole lot better.

***Don't:* Be the textile weaver of the eighteenth century who found himself quickly out of a job, or the shipping company that's still drafting stowage plans with paper and colored pencils.**

***Do:* Be the nimblest, most forward-thinking small business in your niche, by being the first to automate the stuff that used to be costly and tedious.**

What follows is a sampling of just a few powerful, low-cost digital tools to help you do precisely that in seven essential areas of your business. Of course, these technologies are constantly evolving, and new entrants are coming into the market daily. But what follows should help you make a strong start at catapulting your business into the Digital Age.

Scheduling

Most people are still doing scheduling the old fashioned way. It goes something like this.

"Can you do Thursday at one?"

"Ooh, no, sorry. What about four?"

"Shoot, no, that's when I pick up my kids. How about Friday?"

And so on.

Or, best-case scenario, you don't have to use your precious time for scheduling because you're successful enough to have a personal assistant. In other words, you pay someone else good money to do all of that *for* you. Most likely, though, you can't afford a personal assistant.

Now you don't need a spacious budget to outsource scheduling. Artificial intelligence can do it for you. And there's a whole variety of scheduling apps and digital services to handle this. There's **Calendly,** which is an online fixed-calendar system where you set up your preferences and then it automatically syncs to Office 365, Google Calendar, or any other calendar program you choose. That way, it knows your availability, and you can tell it when you want people to schedule times, and for how long, and what kind of buffer you want between appointments. Then, people can just go to the site and book time with you.

But there are even more sophisticated programs entering the market. There's **Amy**—whose website is the mysterious-sounding "x.ai"—in which a polite, Siri-like robot handles your scheduling. It's easy. All you have to do is blind-copy Amy's e-mail address into an e-mail about scheduling, and Amy will automatically respond to your counterpart by saying something like, "That sounds great. When would you like to schedule an appointment? Justin is available at these three times. Do any of those work for you?"

Your counterpart replies, "Yeah, Friday at two works for me."

Amy responds again: "OK, great. It's all set. Thanks."

In other words, it's a personable, friendly system that requires no setup, and automates the entire process. Over the course of weeks and months and years, it will save you untold numbers of hours. **Then you can redirect your valuable time toward making your business better. Why *wouldn't* you use a tool like that?** And we're just getting started.

Document Management

Document management is big. In businesses of every kind, it's astonishing how much time gets wasted just looking for things. It doesn't matter whether your business is general contracting—and you're trying to find a bid you did for a project, or the blueprint for another one, or an invoice you submitted that hasn't been remitted—or you're an attorney, and you're trying to find a brief you need, or a transcription, or an earlier draft of a contract. Whatever your business, document management sucks up a lot of time, and therefore, money.

There was a time when that was necessary—a time when we lived in a paper world, and you could try to be as organized as possible in a paper-filing cabinet, but it just was what it was. You lost time looking for stuff.

But today, that's completely unnecessary. You can go paperless easily and cheaply. Systems like **SharePoint**, **Dropbox**, and **Google Drive**—among others—make document management ultra-easy. These programs give you *at least* the same power that was only available to Fortune 500 companies ten or fifteen years ago. Today, you can have all of your documents indexed, organized, synced, and instantaneously made available to you on every device, from your office computer to your personal phone.

And **if you're *not* managing your documents in the cloud, you're at a disadvantage**. Your competitors are getting wise to this better way of doing business. Meanwhile, the cost of a system like Dropbox or Google Drive is negligible, and it's going to save you materially in time, money, and sanity. Waste not one more second in the obsolete world of paper.

Communication

We used to live in a world where you had a physical office with a physical phone system and a receptionist who just sat there and directed calls. It was expensive. And if that receptionist was on lunch break, or it was after five o'clock, there was no one to route the call. That's just the way it was.

But that's not the world we live in anymore.

The PBX—private branch exchange phone system—has moved into the cloud. There are a number of virtual PBXs now available to you, with **RingCentral** being a great example. They'll represent your small business with every bit of the professionalism as the phone system at a Fortune 500 company. You can have as many extensions as you need—"press one for shipping," "press two for receiving," and so on—or you can have your company's main line ring directly to your personal phone, or you can alternate between the two, depending on day and time. It all depends on what's right for your business. And these systems cost as little as twenty bucks a month.

On top of that, let's say you want to make sure your customers reach a human being every time they call. Expensive, right? Nope.

You can easily connect your virtual PBX to a virtual receptionist like **Ruby Receptionists**. Let's say a customer is calling at ten at night. Or its business hours, but you're in a meeting. It doesn't matter. If you don't want your customer to get a voicemail, you can connect them to a human receptionist who will take their message and get it to you, all at a price point designed for the limited small-business budget. All of a sudden, you can keep your customers happy around the clock, in a way that would have been cost-prohibitive before.

Or consider something like **Olark**, which is for customers who don't want to pick up the phone but who are on your website and would prefer to chat online. Olark allows you to install a "chat with us live" functionality at the bottom of any site for very low cost. And if constantly sitting in front of your computer just in case a random prospect looking at your website decides they want to chat sounds overwhelming to you, you can use the Olark app so that whenever somebody initiates a chat, you get a notification on your smartphone, and then you can reply instantly. In other words, you're always there to answer customer questions, no matter what you're doing. You could be sitting next to a swimming pool sipping a margarita, and you're still serving every customer. Still too much work? Well, there are plenty of companies you can pay to man those chat windows for you at whatever hours you want.

Web Development

Strange as it may seem, Web development is starting to look as quaint as custom tailoring. In the last chapter we talked about how hardly anyone buys a custom suit anymore, since the ones available at Men's Wearhouse are pretty darn good, and you just need a tailor to make some minor alterations after you've selected what you want.

A similar phenomenon is happening in Web development. You can now get a beautiful, highly functional website off the rack from a company like **Squarespace**, **Weebly**, or **Strikingly**, and along with it, you'll get great tech support. The cost is negligible. Meanwhile, **PageCloud** is trying to change the Web development game in terms of customization and flexibility—especially for graphic designers who want more flexibility than a template affords, but who don't know how to write code.

Of course, as CEO of your small business, fussing around on Squarespace or PageCloud to tweak your site is *still* not something you should be doing. But you won't have much trouble finding someone at a very affordable hourly rate to do it for you. You sure won't need a $100-an-hour Web developer, because Squarespace has already done the coding. You *will* need someone who's very Internet literate—say, someone born after 1990—to interface with Squarespace on your behalf for roughly two hours a month. You sure won't have any trouble finding someone who fits that description.

Marketing

In the past, marketing operations could drain endless time from staff at a small business. You typed the same e-mail that you'd typed 200 times before and then sent it off to a customer. But whether in marketing or any other area, if you find yourself or your staff doing that type of repetitive work, odds are there's technology that can automate it. Doing so will add more value to your customers, because **now, you're not wasting time doing stuff that could have been done by a robot while you were sleeping, and instead, you're focused on meeting your customers' needs in ever-greater ways.**

MailChimp, **Infusionsoft**, **Autopilot**, and **HubSpot** are great examples of software that will automate your marketing processes, and new ones are coming out all the time. Let's say somebody comes to your website and subscribes to your blog, or fills out a short form to download a free e-book you offer. An automated message goes out to them welcoming them into your team. It tells them what to expect. From there on out, actions are automatically triggered by other events. So if they pick up the phone, it applies a tag to them, then it automatically sends out another e-mail, or it reminds an employee to do something, or if they purchase something on your website, it automatically sends them a receipt and then adds them to a certain distribution list of existing customers as opposed to prospects.

In other words, marketing software performs whichever functions are necessary within the specific parameters of your business—for pennies.

Employee Management

If history is any indication, tax and regulatory law will become only more complicated in the future. That means the question to ask is, "Will that complexity drain ever more resources from my business, or will I turn it into a competitive advantage by efficiently managing that complexity in a way my competitors aren't?"

It used to be that small-business owners had no choice about dealing personally with HR paperwork. You couldn't afford even a part-time human resources person to do it for you, and the only software out there was designed for huge corporations, with price tags to match. But that's changed, and there are great and highly affordable options available to *you*. Most small-business owners haven't caught on yet, though, and by being among the first to shed this burden you'll be at the helm of a more cost-effective business.

Zenefits offers a completely free human-resources information-systems platform, and it's the sort of thing that, until recently, was only available to very large corporations. Yes, I said completely free. How do they do it? They're also an insurance company. They're hoping you're going to use them to provide benefits to your company. But in doing so, they're giving away tremendously powerful software for you to use for life, whether you ultimately use them for insurance or not.

Back in Chapter Four we talked about PEOs, or professional employer organizations, and the power of outsourcing payroll and benefits. **Justworks** is one example of an organization that will actually become a co-employer with you and serve as the employer of record for the IRS. This is as simple as set it and forget it. Once your PEO is in place, you only manage your employees in terms of their contribution to your business operations. You let someone else handle payroll, benefits, and all the corresponding regulatory and tax laws. The upshot is huge savings for you in time, money, and headaches.

Legal

In the last chapter we talked about how the law profession is changing dramatically, and how lawyers are scared because technology is replacing some of the stuff they used to do. That might be scary for lawyers, but it's unequivocally great news for everyone else.

Rocket Lawyer and **LegalZoom** are sites that connect you instantly with legal services, whether expert advice, document creation, or a legal process like trademarking. There's also **Priori Legal**, which is a network of attorneys who specialize in servicing small businesses and acting as outsourced corporate counsel.

These kinds of websites are changing the legal marketplace at a breakneck pace, and that translates into enormous savings for you. You're probably still in the mindset that any legal expertise is going to cost you well into four digits. Wrong. And you can leverage this trend to your advantage, and become more legal efficient and tax efficient (through a tax-law strategy) than you ever could have been before. **While your competitors are lost in a legal maelstrom, you're sailing to long-term profitability.**

The Twenty-First-Century Assembly Line

Now you've got all the best high-tech tools to do everything that no longer needs to be done by hand. But **how about the ways cutting-edge technology can help you turn a good staff into a winning team? That's ahead.**

11

The New Value Chain: How to Double Your Profits by Making a Simple Tweak to Your Workflow

The invisibility of work and workers in the Digital Age is as consequential as the rise of the assembly line.

—George Packer

(American Journalist)

Do you know what is the all-around most common complaint I hear from small-business owners?

That they can't find good people.

It *is* hard to find good staff; at least, it's hard if you need to trust them with a ton of complex work and you're not able to pay them a whole lot for all that responsibility.

As it turns out, Henry Ford had the same problem. Apparently, it was pretty difficult—maybe even downright impossible—to find a craftsman who could build an automobile from scratch, never mind the fact that Ford couldn't offer much pay if he was going to make cars that were affordable for the everyday consumer while also keeping his operation in the black.

That's precisely when he had his big idea, and the assembly line was born. He realized it wasn't difficult to find good people who could put together component parts as one step in an assembly line that they didn't even have to fully understand, much less, fully execute. Ford's solution was a creative new way of using labor while also harnessing available technology.

And that's exactly what we're doing in this chapter. Just the way the last chapter applied the wisdom of the first Industrial Revolution to automate what used to be done by hand, **we're now going to combine the wisdom of the assembly line with cutting-edge technology in order to fundamentally rethink the way business gets done. The goal is to make your team more efficient, cost-effective, and profitable than ever before.**

Am I saying you should run your business like an assembly line? Actually, yes—though you'll see, over the course of this chapter, that it doesn't mean turning your staff into a team of mindless drones. It's the opposite, actually. **Thanks to technology, your team shouldn't really be doing *any* mindless labor. What should they be doing instead? Helping to grow your business in ways that are specific to their skill sets and your needs.** We'll get to that in a minute, but first, we're going to explore how technology makes it all possible.

The New Value Chain Changes Everything

It used to be that big businesses had a considerable advantage over smaller competitors thanks to their enormous staff. So many employees allowed for very focused specialization—each employee had his or her tiny domain—which was far more efficient than having employees do a little bit of everything. And that efficiency translated into a big advantage.

If that sounds a lot like an assembly line, it's because the fundamental idea is the same. In today's parlance, this is the concept of *breaking up the value chain*—that is, relying on increasingly focused specialists to do very specific tasks, and then putting their work together to yield a less expensive finished product. In the past, only big businesses were able to break up the value chain, because a big staff was a basic ingredient. A small enterprise could never afford it, nor would they have enough specialized work to occupy a full- or even part-time staffer's time. And that's why even ten years ago, this concept was almost irrelevant for small-business owners.

Not anymore.

Technology means you're no longer limited to the confines of your office building, and you no longer need job descriptions substantive enough to justify a commute. These revolutionary changes give you untold flexibility in how to design your workforce and workflow. And I'm not just talking about how e-mail and Skype make it possible for your staff to work from home just as easily as at the physical office. That's certainly true—and there's a remote workforce revolution underway—but I'm talking about something much, much bigger.

I'm talking about what I call the "commoditization of boring."

Entrepreneurs around the world have examined business processes with a fine-tooth comb, looking for tasks being done over and over again by a lot of people. And they're doing that because those tasks represent an opportunity for specialization—for a company to do one little thing, and to do it better than anyone else. They're turning boring, repeatable tasks into a commodity by providing outsourced services, so businesses never have to do those things internally ever again. There are more of these B2B—business-to-business—companies popping up all the time, and they exist for no other reason but to help *your* business outsource boring tasks at a cost of pennies.

The last chapter introduced you to a variety of such companies. I've already mentioned how **Ruby Receptionists** can handle your phone calls. Meanwhile, the company **Bench.co** can do your bookkeeping, and **Zirtual** will provide you with an ultra-efficient personal assistant for a fraction of what you'd pay for even the most part-time staff.

But how about short yet important tasks like sprucing up your website or writing copy for a brochure? Sites like **Upwork** instantly connect you to a pool of tens of thousands of freelancers who perform very specific services—Web design and development, writing, and much more—while also allowing you to see how other business owners have rated their past work.

This directly addresses the number-one concern that I mentioned at the start of the chapter: finding good people. The new paradigm is both quintessentially twenty-first century *and* grounded in Henry Ford's assembly line: It's a lot easier to find good people when you're trusting them with a very specific task, when you can easily see how well they've done in the past, and when you can quickly assess whether or not they're doing satisfactory work for you. That's why Upwork, and other similar sites, makes it easier than ever to get work done efficiently, regardless of how big or small your business is.

In other words, **there's nothing holding you back from creating a workflow that's every bit as intelligent and efficient as one at a Fortune 500 company (or even better). You have a digital universe of affordable human *and* technological resources at your fingertips.**

Making your business competitive in today's marketplace means capitalizing on all those resources, and doing *that* means scrutinizing every link in the value chain of your business down to its smallest component parts. You can then determine the best way to execute each task, and thus design the most efficient workflow, just like Ford did.

For Ford, that meant breaking up every task between designing at the drawing board and putting rubber on the road. For a neighborhood pizza shop, the process of breaking up the value chain might look entirely different, though the underlying wisdom is the same. And when I founded my international shipping company several years ago, I used the same logic in order to dissect the traditional job of a vessel planner. I saw the standard job description in our industry had experts spending a lot of time sending e-mail and only a little time on the high-value work of drafting stowage plans. I broke up the process: I created a part-time administrative position for handling e-mail, then had the experts focus on creating great stowage plans at a fraction of the cost of our competitors.

Whatever your business and whatever your current workflow, separate your processes into as many bite-sized steps as you possibly can. Then examine each of the steps and ask yourself the following:

1. **How often are we doing this task?**
2. **How much time does it take?**
3. **Who's doing it?**
4. **At what cost?**

This is your business's essential machinery. Once mapped, you can bring in all the possibility the Digital Revolution affords you:

5. **Given the options of in-house versus outsourcing, automation, or some combination of the above, what is *the most efficient way* to perform this task?**

With this line of questioning, and a commitment to designing the best workflow possible, you're on your way to outcompeting a sea of small businesses that are stuck doing things the old way.

You're also on your way to outcompeting those who adopt every shiny new bell and whistle without strategy or analysis. Indeed, technology isn't always cheaper. Sometimes the least expensive means is manual; that's most often the case when we're talking about a task that takes only an hour or two a month. I've seen business owners get so excited about the newest, hottest piece of technology that they drop tens of thousands of dollars on a gismo that will save them an hour a month. At that rate, it will take them a decade for the investment to pay off, and by the time you consider all the front-end work to get the automated system going, it just isn't worth it. **The point of technology is to give you the freedom and flexibility to design the most cost-effective workflow possible, not to use every technological innovation at whatever the cost.**

Man or Machine? The Case of Amazon's Mechanical Turk

"Automated" is a fuzzy word. Regardless of whether it's a machine or a human doing the work, a task probably feels automated to you as long as you're not doing it yourself. And for good reason.

In 2005, Amazon launched a site called Mechanical Turk, whose purpose was to attract a human workforce to handle tasks that couldn't be done by a computer. Soon, thousands of people flocked to the site, and today, the Mechanical Turk workforce has surpassed half a million. And it's no longer just Amazon posting jobs—known as HITs, or Human Intelligence Tasks—on the site. Lots of other businesses do too.

Mechanical Turk is hugely popular, but not because it's some kind of fancy automation. The work being done is completely manual. What's important is that it represents the best means by which businesses can execute particular tasks. As with all business processes, what matters isn't how high- or low-tech the solution. Instead, it's how cost-effective the means, and how it helps your business do what it does, better.

The Golden Formula Meets Workforce Development

No matter how much you outsource, or how many great digital resources you have to automate different parts of your business, you're still going to need great people. You need someone to do the essential work of finding and engaging the necessary resources and overseeing them on your behalf. There was an endless supply of labor to work on Henry Ford's assembly line, screwing pieces together, but what about someone to *design* the assembly line and to ensure it worked smoothly? Well, that's why you've got your expert outsourced COO.

And a good thing, too, because our next move will require all the expertise of your COO *and* the rest of your team. With all the mindless work dispatched as efficiently as humanly (or technologically) possible, it's now time to identify and elevate the best and highest skill set of each of your team members.

Back at the beginning of the book, we introduced the Golden Formula, and we've been returning to it again and again. We built that formula on three fundamental questions:

- Where am I spending my time?
- What is the cost of my labor?
- How much value am I adding to my business?

These questions don't just apply to your work as CEO. They also apply to each of your employees.

What unique skills and value does your staff have? How can you maximize the value they add to your business in those areas of skill? One of the most important responsibilities you have as CEO is building a great team, and technology doesn't change that one iota.

People were afraid in the 1980s that computers were going to replace people, and some of the same fears have resurfaced in the digital wave. But, **as a small-business owner, digital technology isn't—and *absolutely should not be*—your ticket to downsizing great employees. On the contrary, it's your chance to give talented team members ever-greater opportunity to add tremendous value to your business through their unique skills.**

Hopefully, this jives with your own instinct, because I'll bet you've got someone—or, if you're lucky, several people—on your team whom you trust, and who you know have great potential. Maybe you were reading all this stuff about "breaking up the value chain" and you were thinking, *I have some great employees; I don't want to take work away from them!*

Good instinct.

What you've got is trust capital; you've got employees who are smart and dedicated, and you trust them to do good work. That trust capital is every bit as valuable as financial capital, if not more so, because it's harder to come by. So when you've found it, you don't take it for granted. That's just smart.

So how do you break up the value chain *and* keep your talented team members busy?

For starters, not everything in your back office can be deconstructed and outsourced to super-specialized experts, as we just mentioned. You still need people to manage the assembly line to make sure all the component parts are put together smoothly. But far beyond that, there are things that are critical to the voice and image of your company. Here's where we start to harness your employees' great potential.

Indeed, even after every cost-saving technological innovation, there's *plenty* of work left for your talented employees. It's just not the same work as before—and that's a good thing. It's work that will allow them to add more value to your company, and to feel more fulfilled as a result. Just the way you and LeBron James do better work when you're performing your passion, your employees will too. They come to work every day for a paycheck, of course, but that's not the only thing motivating them—and all of us— as human beings. Each of us wants the opportunity to feel fruitful; each of us wants to feel that we're doing meaningful work in the world. You're about to give your team that chance.

Maybe all of this sounds a little too theoretical. So let's look at a specific example. Let's go back to Jim, our lawyer friend who's at the helm of his own law firm.

Let's say Jim hired an associate attorney—someone fresh out of law school—in order to "break up the value chain" and delegate some of the simpler legal work to someone else. But since there aren't a full 2,000 hours of legal work for this younger lawyer to do, she actually does a mix of attorney and paralegal work. And though she's only been at the law firm for a year, Jim sees her very much as a core employee. He has trust capital with her and wants to invest in her for the future.

Now let's say Jim *also* has a paralegal working for him. The paralegal does a mix of things, from some bread-and-butter paralegal stuff to legal-secretarial tasks, transcription, bookkeeping, and basic filing. And though Jim is happy with the paralegal work this guy does, he doesn't have much trust capital with him. That's because the paralegal, in contrast to the associate attorney, takes a lot of cigarette breaks and spends quite a bit of time on Facebook.

There's nothing unusual about this scenario, of course. This situation, and similar ones, play out in just about every small business in every industry every day.

So what should Jim do in order to get the most out of his team?

First of all, since the paralegal is spending time on filing, it means this firm still hasn't gone completely paperless. So Jim takes care of that. In the last chapter, we talked about a few digital tools for document management. The important thing is to move *everything* into the cloud, thereby saving a tremendous amount of time and money.

Once that's done, Jim is no longer limited to a talent pool in his local vicinity. That will allow him to break up the value chain.

He outsources to a receptionist service, a bookkeeper, a transcriptionist, and a legal secretary. And, of course, the filing that the paralegal used to do has been eliminated, since everything's paperless. The paralegal now has nothing on his plate but the core paralegal work.

Remember that the associate attorney was also doing some paralegal work, so Jim now moves *all* paralegal work to the paralegal. Now it's easier to track what he's doing and, in many cases, bill that work out to clients. Boy, is that a change for the better! But here's an even bigger change: Jim now shifts the paralegal from a full-time salary to an hourly system, in which he's only paid for his actual time worked (no more time on Facebook). The lawyer saves money, even as he *raises* the paralegal's hourly rate above what it was in the old salary.

Meanwhile, the associate, who's a promising young attorney, doesn't have a full workload anymore since she lost her paralegal responsibilities. So what now?

Jim starts sending her to conferences, where she's networking on behalf of the firm and sharpening her own legal acumen. She's *also* now in charge of the firm's blog *and* she starts ghostwriting articles for her boss—an arrangement that raises the firm's profile and lets her develop still more expertise in complicated legal theory.

And what's the result of all this musical chairs?

Without adding one dollar of revenue, the firm just doubled its bottom-line net profits.

Prior to these changes, the firm was pulling in just shy of $300,000 per year. That translated to a salary of $120,000 for Jim, $80,000 for the associate, and $65,000 for the paralegal, with about $15,000 in profit left over.

In this new scenario, the lawyer and the associate stay at the same salaries, and the lawyer has to pay around $15,000 for the new specialists (the outsourced receptionist, the bookkeeper, and so on). Meanwhile, the paralegal now only pulls in about $35,000.

That leaves $30,000 in net profits—fully *double* the previous amount.

But even more exciting than this immediate cash benefit, Jim has also substantially improved his firm's marketing strategy with the new time investment from the associate, who's busy writing and networking and providing thought leadership in a way that will surely increase their revenue over time. And for each new revenue dollar that comes, more of it is profit, since they have a more efficient and streamlined operation.

Not to mention the fact that the associate is much, much happier. She didn't go to law school to spend her time on paralegal work—and now, not only has she chucked that from her workload, she's also being challenged and used to her maximum potential. That means she's far less likely to leave the firm for greener pastures since she loves what she's doing and she's building a great resume. Not to mention the fact that, as we've talked about more than once, there's an efficiency to passion that greatly enhances her output.

But what about that paralegal? He got reduced from full-time to part-time. Surely, he's the loser in this situation, right? Wrong.

He got bumped to a higher hourly rate, and he's now working half the hours he used to. So what did he do with all that spare time? He took another part-time job at a different law firm. And now he's happier than ever, because he hated filing and transcription, and now he's doing only high-value paralegal work. At the higher hourly rate, spread across two firms, he's now making $75,000 instead of $65,000. Not to mention the fact that he has more job security, since, if something happens to one firm, he's only 50 percent out of a job and won't have much trouble picking up work at another firm. That security is nice to have in the small-business world. Most of all, though, the paralegal is just happier. He likes what he's doing and he—like the associate attorney—is now being challenged.

Win, win, win.

Sounds too good to be true, doesn't it: a win-win-win scenario in which nobody loses? That's just not how the world works, right?

But that's the power of efficiency and the cost of waste. It's why the Industrial Revolution was so powerful, and it's why the Digital Revolution is changing everything.

The Secret Weapon of the Small Business

Hopefully, you're now a digital convert, and you're ready and eager to put all the goods of the Digital Age to use making your business better than it's ever been.

But wait! There's even *more* good news.

In the Digital Age, small businesses don't just compete against much bigger ones in ways that were impossible before. It's even better than that. Small businesses often have an *advantage* over their much larger peers.

How can that be? Read on.

12

Leveling the Playing Field: Why Small Is Big in the Digital Age

Giants are not what we think they are.
The same qualities that appear to give them
strength are often the sources of great weakness.

—Malcolm Gladwell
(Canadian Writer)

You've now read all about the ways in which big companies used to squash their smaller competitors. They used to have the best technology—which small businesses could never afford—*and* they used their human workforce more efficiently, by breaking up the value chain in a way small businesses couldn't. You also now know that those big-business advantages have largely dissolved. All the formerly expensive tools and strategies that used to give the big guy an edge are now available to you, the small-business CEO, at the click of a mouse or the swipe of your finger.

But that's not the whole story. In today's world, it's not just that big businesses no longer have a leg up. It's *also* the case that small businesses have a couple important advantages over their much larger peers. One such advantage is on the left side of your Business Model Canvas, while the other is on the right.

Our task in this chapter? To help you leverage *both* sides of your canvas to put your business in a position of strength relative to competitors of any size, shape, and location.

David and Goliath

As a small-business owner, it can be intimidating to think of competing with a huge corporation. For one thing, every corporation sits atop complex infrastructure. There are enormous office buildings that house hundreds of workers; there's the intricate, custom IT systems; and there are whole divisions for HR and legal, to keep talent coming in the corporate door and to keep lawsuits at bay.

This infrastructure used to underlie the big-business advantages you just read about—namely, it was precisely that expensive infrastructure that allowed corporations to make use of the very best technology and to design the most efficient internal workflows.

But the consumerization of technology that you read about in Chapter Ten changed all that, since workers at the base of the corporate pyramid now come to work carrying iPads that are more powerful than their employer's sprawling and costly IT systems. At the same time, as you read in Chapter Eleven, small businesses can now use cutting-edge tools to design internal workflows every bit as efficient (or more so!) than those of big corporations.

So that infrastructure has now changed from a valuable advantage into a considerable *dis*advantage. Think of it like a vast container ship out on the ocean. This ship is over one thousand feet long and can carry ten thousand tons of cargo. And now, let's say there's a sea change, and the ship needs to shift direction. How quickly can it turn? Slow as molasses—it may well take half a mile for that ship to change course.

Big corporations have spent millions on systems and infrastructure, and they can't just flush it all down the toilet on a whim. It's too hard to replace, and there's too much riding on it. But that means integrating new technology and keeping up with the rapid pace of change is a lot more difficult for a very large company than a small one. The story of Hewlett-Packard and Dell is a famous example of this.

Before Dell's arrival in the PC market, companies like Hewlett-Packard relied on big-box stores as the essential distribution channel for their products. Then Dell showed up with a different way of doing things: Dell went straight to the customer and built computers to order. This was revolutionary. Meanwhile, HP saw what its smaller competitor was doing, but it had a vast infrastructure designed for an entirely different kind of product delivery, and couldn't change that overnight. By the time HP execs tried to compete on these new terms, Dell had carved out a sizable share of the market.

Fast-forward to today. What company could symbolize market dominance better than Apple, whose products are literally everywhere you look? Yet Apple is scared. Apple is continuously buying up small companies because its executives don't want anyone to get big enough to become a threat, the way Dell did to HP. Despite its seemingly unassailable dominance, Apple knows that a nimble start-up could change the game. So the company buys up smaller ones and then shuts them down. Meanwhile, Google and Facebook do the very same thing.

Then there's the human side of all that corporate infrastructure. A big company has layer upon layer of management, which brings with it a heavy inertia. Each manager has a particular domain to oversee, and everyone falls into a mindset of protecting his or her own small fiefdom, rather than focusing on the business as a whole. Talk about a ship that's hard to turn.

And that's precisely why you now see companies like Microsoft participating in the Lean Startup Conference. Microsoft and other big companies realize that if they can't develop a culture that mimics the nimbleness of start-ups, it might be the end of them. For that reason, plenty of Fortune 500 companies create subsidiaries and spin-offs with an intentionally different kind of culture—so they can pivot while keeping their big steamships from hitting an iceberg.

Meanwhile, your small business can speed across the water like a jet ski or a speedboat, and turn on a dime. And so while big businesses are scared, you should feel empowered. It doesn't matter if you're a tech company with sights on a billion-dollar market or if you're a local pizza shop. In either case, there's a Goliath after the same market you are—and *you* have valuable assets to bring to the table.

On the top of the list is your ability to keep your operation efficient and lean, since big-business infrastructure represents a whole lot of costly overhead. In today's world, overhead adds increasingly less value while draining the bottom line, whereas you have the ability to utilize the best technology and design your workforce and workflow with razor-sharp efficiency. In other words, **successfully competing against a much larger competitor means exploiting all the advantages of being small and dexterous. This strategy is as old as David and Goliath, and as new as the latest app. Your job is to harness all the cutting-edge resources and processes that we've covered in the last couple chapters, so that you're truly the speedboat zipping past the ocean liner**.

That may well sound far-fetched if you're at the helm of a business that has just a couple employees. But the trends are on your side. In industries as vast as media and law and from hotels to transportation to international shipping, the rules are rapidly changing. The old guard is terrified. You can ride the digital wave and outlast not only your small to midsize competitors, but also vast corporations, by making your small business as nimble as it can be.

David and . . . David

Everything in this chapter thus far has had to do with the left side of your Business Model Canvas. We've been focused on the value of small-business efficiency in the Digital Age. But perhaps the greatest advantage of a small business over a much larger one has nothing to do with efficiency, and instead, lives on the *right* side of your canvas—in the value that you provide to your customer.

Ever needed assistance from a big company and gotten lost in a maze of automated recordings? Of course you have, and there are few things as frustrating. As a small-business owner, you can provide your customers with an alternative to such big-business agony.

Indeed, your small business offers a value that's entirely separate from the product you provide. You have the ability to create one-on-one customer relationships in a way that large companies absolutely cannot. However much your big competitors love to talk about customer service, sheer volume has forced them to do things like set up offshore call centers. When a customer is lucky enough to get an actual human being on the phone, the person on the other end of the line—however competent and well meaning—cannot offer a personal connection or establish an ongoing relationship based on mutual trust. That matters in a big way.

In fact, there's a ton of research on this very issue, and it squarely indicates that people prefer doing business with others from their own community—that is, we prefer doing business with people like ourselves. Without straying too far into the weeds of sociology, studies suggest that in business as well as other areas of life, we prefer to use local networks rather than relying on outsiders.[16] Sellers and buyers in local markets follow their own specific social norms, and long-term associations subsequently emerge, fostering strong ties between them.[17]

The reason isn't abstract. We share interests and values with our local peers. We have the same ideas about how business should be conducted, and we may even know some of the same people.[18,19]

These things create a sense of trust, and that's the basic recipe for forming acquaintanceships and relationships. So it's our natural preference to turn to people like ourselves when we need a product or service, and that preference and mutual exchange then serve as the basis for an ongoing connection.

In other words, your small business is the perfect environment for building trust capital between you and your customer base. It's something that customers will pay for, and it will keep them coming back again and again. At the same time, big corporations just can't compete.

Let's say you're a small-town pizza shop, and I live down the street from you. When I walk into your shop, you say hello and remember my name. You've also prominently displayed a photo of the local little league team that you're supporting, and I see my friend's kid in the picture. What's more, you're working with a local food bank to provide dinner for local food-insecure families. So when I pay for my pizza I have the option of putting a couple dollars toward dinner for a nearby family who otherwise might go hungry. These people are my neighbors, and that has value to me. It's not the same value as providing a delicious pizza; it's a *social* value. And I'm willing to pay for it. I have a relationship with you, the shop owner, and through that relationship, I feel more connected to my community. The upshot? When Pizza Hut opens down the street and says they'll deliver, *and* their pizzas are five-dollars cheaper, I don't care. I'm not willing to go to the chain establishment. The social value of going to my neighborhood shop is well worth five bucks.

Or consider a real-life pizza shop I came across in a small town in a very rural area. Of course, the shop is owned by a local family, and everyone knows everyone's name. The interior of the restaurant has old-fashioned wallpaper and a table with board games, plus the local newspaper is always scattered around for everyone to share. There are homemade soups and chocolate-chip cookies displayed on a sideboard; they were prepared that morning and are absolutely delicious. And there's a chalkboard on one wall. On the chalkboard is a listing of recent wildlife sightings, and anyone can add to it. So when you come in to get your dinner, you notice that one of your neighbors saw a bald eagle, and someone else saw a blue heron, and someone else spotted a bear and two cubs. You feel connected to your community in an unusual way.

Of course that kind of thing wouldn't make any sense in most places—and that's the point. In this tiny community in this very rural place, there is shared interest in what sort of wildlife everyone has seen recently. And that's something Pizza Hut could never know and could never imitate—or, if they tried, they'd fail, because everyone would see right through the big corporation's transparent attempt at acting "local." Not to mention that the whole town is fiercely loyal to their local pizza shop, and for good reason.

That might sound like a really unusual case. You might think this sort of thing only makes sense in a small-town setting. But consider that I'm currently working with a budding entrepreneur who's opening a bar in Brooklyn, New York. That's a competitive market. You've got Applebee's, you've got Buffalo Wild Wings, you've got TGI Friday's, and a million other establishments all competing against each other for the bar crowd. How on earth is my client going to stand out in Brooklyn?

The answer will involve creating a unique culture for a community that is, itself, unique. It will mean having small-batch craft whiskeys, because in that particular market, people love to find something unusual and craft-made. It will mean fostering a bar culture that feels fun. It means providing the right ambiance, the right decor. This is the same idea as a chalkboard with wildlife sightings: Your job as the small-business owner is to create a particular social value for your particular clientele.

Or remember all the way back in Chapter Two, when I described an entrepreneur who's opening a liquor store in the Williamsburg neighborhood of Brooklyn? We were talking about the efficiency of passion, and how this entrepreneur should stay focused on his expertise in order to curate an excellent liquor selection. Now, when it comes to social value, that expertise becomes all the more important. How will his store provide something unique in the crowded market of Williamsburg liquor stores?

Well, perhaps he'll decide he needs to focus on liquor tastings. Perhaps he'll conclude that, for this market, he needs to have an expert on hand all the time who can help customers discover little-known craft liquors and other niche products. And he might rotate his stock more than most, so customers feel like they're constantly discovering something new. That would be a really unusual model for a liquor store; most liquor stores just keep churning out the same stock over and over. So maybe this represents an important dimension for his particular business model. When this entrepreneur started out, he thought he was just selling liquor. But over time, he might realize that, in fact, he's selling an experience.

That might sound like a completely different philosophy from a chalkboard of wildlife sightings, but they're grounded in the same logic. As a small-business owner, you have the opportunity to create a niche experience for your customers: an experience that's designed for, and shaped by, their specific tastes and interests. This doesn't have to be geographically focused. If your business is entirely online, you're still serving a particular group of customers. In either case, it's essential to ask the following: **What's unique about my customers, and how can I—as their peer—deliver a product that has social value in addition to functional value? What social value can I offer that a larger competitor could never provide?**

Remember that big businesses are scared, and that you're in a strong position. Indeed, **you're uniquely positioned to form long-term bonds with your customers, and to create a personal and meaningful experience for them. That, in turn, fosters loyalty, and will put your business in an enviable position of security and sustainability.**

From Riding the Wave to Getting into the Weeds

So at this point in the book, you've escaped the DIY trap, built your C-suite, created a masterpiece Business Model Canvas, and seized all the tools and tactics of the Digital Age to put your small business on the path to success.

But it's likely that you still have some questions nagging at you. You've got questions about raising start-up capital, and whether you should form an LLC, and how to manage your day-to-day calendar to preserve your sanity. These are the most practical, in-the-weeds-type questions. And **in the next and final section of this book, you'll find answers.**

PART IV

PRACTICAL ANSWERS TO THE QUESTIONS SMALL-BUSINESS OWNERS ARE ASKING

How do I build a budget for my small business? Should I form a sole proprietorship or an LLC? How can I manage my time better?

There are certain questions that are always on the minds of small-business owners. This section is the FAQ you've been looking for, applying the wisdom of the previous chapters to the nitty-gritty, day-to-day life of the entrepreneur.

In this section you'll find:

1. How to budget for your business.
2. Tips for funding your business when you're first starting out.
3. What you need to know about corporate formation, from LLCs to C corps, and how (and when) to decide which structure is right for you.
4. How to attract customers and grow your customer base.
5. How to improve your personal time management.
6. And the biggest question of all: how to find that elusive work–life balance.

13

Plan: Questions about Business Plans and Budgeting

By failing to prepare, you are preparing to fail.

—Benjamin Franklin
(American Writer, Inventor,
and Statesman, 1706–1790)

By now, I hope this book has helped to free you from the DIY trap (as we covered in Part I), to refocus your time and energy on designing and growing a profitable business (Part II), and to position that business for success in the changing landscape of our Digital Age (Part III). Now **it's time to turn to some of the most practical, nuts-and-bolts questions facing entrepreneurs and small-business owners.**

In addition to providing some important guidance about questions that every business owner faces, **this section is also meant to help you ask the *right* questions.** We've spent plenty of time talking about how the excitement of starting a business can lead newly minted entrepreneurs to rush through important parts of the planning process; that's why Sue's Bagels in Part II used the wisdom *slow is fast* during the business-development process. So, in addition to answering some of the burning questions that I regularly hear from small-business owners, the final chapters of this book are also intended to help you prioritize, by focusing on some of the most crucial steps to launching a successful business. In this chapter, we'll tackle three common questions:

1. **How do I write a business plan?**
2. **How do I create and use a Business Model Canvas?**
3. **How do I budget for my business?**

How Do I Write a Business Plan?

From Chapter Five you know that you don't necessarily *need* a business plan— and if you don't need one, you certainly don't want to spend dozens of hours writing a lengthy plan that may have little practical value. My default answer to this question is most commonly, "you don't." I then try to redirect the question to a discussion about the Business Model Canvas instead.

That said, there are two common situations in which you really *do* need a business plan: applying for a Small Business Administration loan, and seeking venture capital funding.

A Business Plan for the SBA Loan Application

If you're applying for an SBA loan, I recommend using special software to guide you through the process. Doing so will give you a finished business plan that conforms exactly to what the loan committee expect to see. My personal favorite is LivePlan (http://www.liveplan.com/).

Ideally you've already completed your Business Model Canvas before trying to write a formal business plan (and we'll dig deeper into *that* process in a second). If that's the case, fleshing out your canvas into a long-form business plan should be relatively straightforward. The LivePlan software will allow you to put lots of words (and charts, as appropriate) to the information you already have in sticky notes on your canvas, in order to create precisely the type of plan that you need for the SBA application.

A Business Plan for Seeking Venture Capital

The process of seeking venture capital is more complicated than the SBA application, though the first step is the same. Start by turning your Business Model Canvas into a formal business plan using the LivePlan software I just mentioned.

Then bring in a consultant. Yes, that's right; you most likely need a consultant to help you. The VC process is an inside-ball-game world, and unless you have your own expertise in it, you will need someone who lives and breathes that world in order to increase your chances of actually getting funded, because a consultant will know *exactly* what your potential funders want to see. And if your business truly is a candidate for venture capital, then investing in such a consultant is likely to have a very high ROI; it's the difference between potentially garnering millions of dollars in outside funding or zero.

Ultimately, however, a business plan is just a document designed to explain your business *model*—in this case, for the purpose of convincing them that you have a business model that's viable and investable. But you can't explain something you haven't mapped out for yourself. Furthermore, your business model will be a lot less persuasive to potential investors if it hasn't been tested and verified in any meaningful way yet. That's why, while "How do I write a business plan" is the more common question I hear small business owners asking, the first question *all* small business owners should ask is actually, "How do I create and use a Business Model Canvas?"

How Do I Create and Use a Business Model Canvas?

Whether you're doing a Business Model Canvas for a business that's been operating for a while or for one that's just a kernel of an idea, it's easy to put together a canvas that's primarily based on hopes and assumptions. On top of that, it's easy to shortchange the areas of the canvas that require the most attention—your Value Proposition and Customer Segments, principally—and then put all of your focus on areas that can only really be developed *after* you've nailed your Value Proposition.

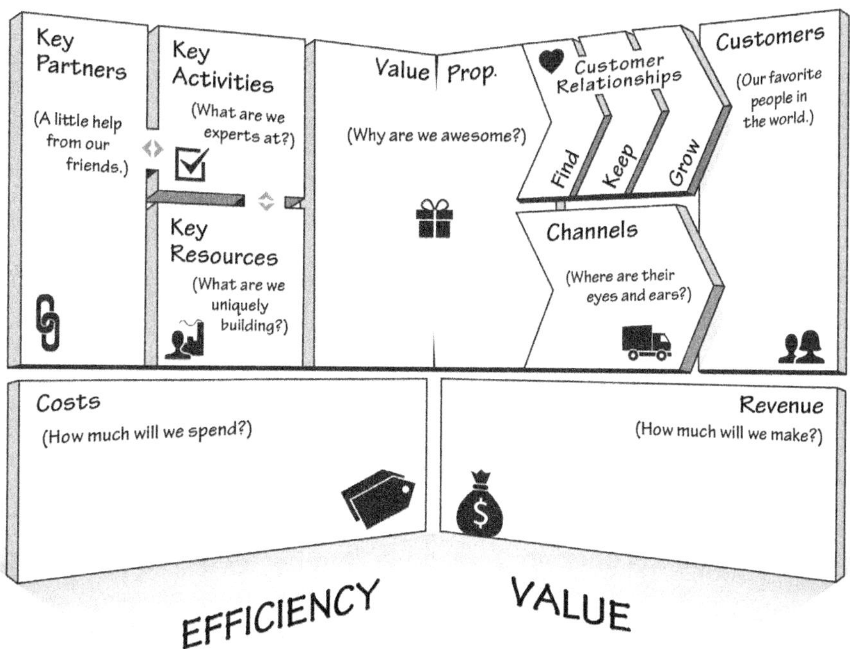

A frequent misstep, for instance, is focusing on Customer Relationships—the question of how to get, keep, and grow your customer base—even before establishing Value Proposition and product-market fit. So let me say in no uncertain terms that **establishing Value Proposition and Customer Segments is your first priority—and together, those two areas of your canvas are your product-market fit.** Remember that **"product-market fit" means you've got a product that satisfies a need or a want in your target market, and that your target market can support your business.**

That raises an important question: How do you know when you've got product-market fit?

I'm glad you asked. **You know you've got product-market fit when you've tested the market and collected data to prove it.**

To do so, build a first draft of your Business Model Canvas. Then ask yourself: **What are the riskiest assumptions on this canvas? Which assumptions—if they turn out to be wrong—will change everything? Which assumptions have the power to invalidate everything else on the canvas?**

Then test those assumptions. Devise creative and cost-effective strategies for testing, in order to convert your assumptions into facts. Test, collect data, and then return to your canvas and revise. Repeat. As you slowly replace conjecture with fact, other assumptions on your canvas will move to the top of your list as the riskiest, and you'll test those too, until you have a business model built on the solid bedrock of fact.

If this sounds onerous, remember that *the number-one reason* start-ups fail is because they were building a product no one wanted. In other words, you're testing product-market fit to keep yourself from going deep in debt and wasting years of your life on a failing venture. If that's not a good enough reason to do some diligent testing, I don't know what is. Indeed, **you're doing nothing less than creating the core of your business. Remember that your *product* isn't the core of your business; your *business model* is.**

Back in Chapter Six, we tracked the progress of Sue's Bagels from her initial plan to (1) provide quality bagels, (2) to a discerning customer base via (3) a physical storefront. Then it turned out that the market cared about convenience, not quality, and thus there was no "discerning" customer base, and a storefront would create little or no value for those customers (while breaking the bank with associated expenses). In other words, *all* of Sue's initial assumptions turned out to be incorrect—and that changed *every single element* of her canvas.

The very same thing may happen to you, and that may sound unpleasant. But you don't have to go through this process alone. I strongly recommend having an outsourced COO in your C-suite, as I wrote in Chapter Four, even before you launch your new business—to help you with this very process.

Now take a moment to commend yourself. If you've just done the hard work of creating a Business Model Canvas that's built on testing and data instead of conjecture, then you're already head and shoulders above the competition—and you've probably just saved yourself from the single most common problem that leads start-ups down the road to failure.

Of course, the *second* most common reason start-ups fail is that they run out of money. Which brings us to our next question:

How Do I Budget for My Business?

There's a place for optimism in entrepreneurship—a big place—but budgeting isn't it. It's all too easy to fantasize about the millions of dollars of revenue that will pour into your coffers, and to gloss over some of the key expenses that are necessary to make even half of that revenue a reality. Thus, **the best approach to budgeting for your small business is to plan for the worst. I promise that such pessimism serves your business's best interests, because its very survival is at stake.**

Let's start with the basics though. It makes sense to think about your budget in terms of your Business Model Canvas, in which all of your revenue is reflected on the right side of the canvas, and all of your costs, on the left. Creating a budget means turning the concepts on your canvas into numbers.

To do so, you need a budgeting tool. You can use the built-in budgeting templates in Microsoft Excel (just click "New" and then search for "budget"), or you can find a free template online. Or if you already have accounting software, you can use that. Keep in mind that it doesn't matter how your budget *looks*. In fact, the fancier it appears, the more likely you are to take it for fact, when the truth is that it's really a lot of guesswork. Thus what matters here is the quality of the data you put into your budget, and the quality of the analysis you pull out of it—but *never* how it looks.

And as with the process of building a Business Model Canvas, it's useful to have a partner in your C-suite to help you with this process. An outsourced CFO is ideal. You can also tap your own network of colleagues, friends, or your spouse to act as a sounding board as you try to think through the assumptions underlying the numbers you put into your budget. The more accurate your guesses, the better off you'll be. So, following are some tips to help you dial in the data.

Revenue

If I told you there was some secret formula for accurately projecting revenue for a new business, I'd be lying through my teeth (or keyboard). Unless you're a fortune-teller, you just can't forecast the amount of money a new business is going to put into its cash register.

That's why, if you're just starting out, the best you can do for the revenue side of your budget is to comb thorough market research and then add a strong dose of pessimism. Use Google to research average revenue figures for businesses similar to yours that service a similar customer demographic. Then ask around; talk to other small-business owners and people in your field. Draw on any past experience. And then take your findings from all that research and *cut it in half*—at least for the first iteration of your budget. Assume it will take you twice as long as you think it will to hit those numbers. If your revenue assumptions ultimately prove to be too conservative, that's great. In that case, you'll have extra money to invest in your more-successful-than-expected business. But what if those pessimistic assumptions turn out to be correct? What if, as is the case with so many start-ups, revenue starts as a trickle and doesn't show much growth for a long time? Well, you're prepared.

This cuts to the underlying purpose of budgeting: **You have a budget for the completely practical purpose of getting you through the next twelve months.** That's twelve months in the real world—not twelve months on paper or in a business plan. Your budget is meant to help you plan and prepare for what lies ahead so you can beat the odds and stay in business when so many others fail.

And if you're just starting out, it's important to acknowledge that you're not going to conquer the world—or your market niche—in your first year. Your business may well not turn a profit in its first twelve months; in fact, that's been the case for nearly every Silicon Valley start-up in history. And that's why you've got a budget. **Your budget is your road map through those initial lean months and years; it's the tool that lets you plan for the *worst* part of starting a business, so you can survive long enough to experience the *best* part of starting a business.**

On the brighter side, budgeting will become easier over time. The longer you're in business, the easier it becomes. Once you've been operating for a little while, you've got some real data; you're no longer making wild guesses. And then you can make projections about the future based on the best possible material: actual historical revenue, coupled with estimates for growth that are consistent with your established trend line.

Costs

The cost side of your budget is just as important as the revenue side, but much easier to calculate.

Start by adding up all the expenses implied on the left side of your Business Model Canvas. Then ask Google, colleagues, other small-business owners, friends, and anyone you can for sample budgets and expenses that may be relevant to your new venture. I can guarantee that there will be expenses that a second (or third, or fourth) pair of eyes will help you identify that you wouldn't otherwise have included (payroll taxes are a common example).

Once you've listed your foreseeable expenses, it's pretty easy to get specific about how much each one will cost. Rent, IT, salaries—these are all knowable. Do your research and plug in the numbers.

Then take a moment to consider how your costs are going to change as your business grows. Some costs will stay the same, while others will grow at the same pace as your revenue. Here's a guide:

- **Fixed Costs:** As the name implies, fixed costs don't change, regardless of how many widgets you sell. Put things like rent, leased furniture, and insurance in this category. These costs are a big hurdle that your business needs to clear; that is, you need a certain amount of revenue to pay for all this stuff. But once you're consistently earning enough to cover fixed costs, profit can grow quickly.

- **Variable Costs:** Variable costs increase as your revenue increases. Put inventory and cost of goods sold (COGS) here.
- **Semi-Variable Costs:** These costs sit somewhere in between the first two. Semi-variable costs remain fixed up until a certain point and then start to grow. Put salaries and certain IT expenses here.

By considering which of your costs fall into these three categories, you can make better projections about how expenses will shift a few months down the road. And now you've made the best possible effort at nailing down the cost side of your budget.

The Big Picture

Once you've got both sides of your budget in place, you have a sense of your projected profits:

Revenue – Costs = Profit

Many start-ups (and virtually all tech start-ups) don't turn a profit in the first year, so don't panic if your budget doesn't show a profit. In fact, you're already on stronger footing than many new entrepreneurs, who manipulate the numbers until their budget is in the black, and then fail to prepare for the alternative.

Once you've been in business for a while, you can draw on your budget for key insights into your business. An important one is profit margin:

Profit / Revenue = Profit Margin

Your profit margin is a percentage of your revenue; specifically, it tells you what percentage of your revenue is profit. That's a basic insight that comes from a budget. With the help of an outsourced

CFO, you can use your budget to draw countless other insights about your business to learn from mistakes, reduce costs, and grow your profit margin in the future. And a good CFO will help you develop a set of Key Performance Indicators (KPIs) to help with goal-setting and tracking progress, as well as creating employee incentives and measuring employee performance.

Finally, remember that your budget should change and evolve as your business does; in order for it to be useful to you, your budget can be no more static than the business itself. Continue to update it as new information comes to light, because **a good budget is one of the most important and powerful tools in the small-business owner's toolbox.**

Putting Plans into Action

Now you've taken the time to develop a smart Business Model Canvas, and you've done the hard work of mapping out a budget. So it's time to put all that planning to work. And for most entrepreneurs, that raises questions about corporate formation and funding. We'll tackle those next.

14

Start: Questions about Corporate Formation and Funding

Don't start a company unless it's an obsession and something you love. If you have an exit strategy, it's not an obsession.

—Mark Cuban

(Serial Entrepreneur, Billionaire, and Investor)

It might not be the sexiest of all subjects, but the choice between forming a C corporation or a Limited Liability Company (among other options) will have far-reaching effects for your business. It's worth getting right the first time. Facebook founder Mark Zuckerberg famously incorporated his business as a Florida-based LLC when just about every other tech entrepreneur in Silicon Valley was forming as a Delaware C corporation (soon I'll explain why), and that decision ended up creating a lot of problems for him. So don't be like Mark Zuckerberg—in the arena of corporate formation, that is.

In the pages ahead, I'll define your key options for corporate structure, from sole proprietorship to C corp. Then I'll pose some important questions that you should ask yourself in order to determine which structure is right for you. I'll also raise a few flags and clear up some common points of confusion. And once we've covered all of that, **we'll then turn to funding strategies—that is, how to attract capital for your new enterprise**.

The Many Choices for Corporate Structure

The following are the five most common corporate structures chosen by entrepreneurs. Let's start with some basic definitions:

Sole Proprietorship

This is the most basic structure. As the name implies, the owner alone is responsible for the company and all of its liabilities and assets. All profits or losses are recorded on the owner's personal tax return, and the owner pays self-employment tax on any money received. A sole proprietorship does *not* require registration with the secretary of state.

General Partnership

In a general partnership, two or more owners share ownership of the business. Partners share in the decision-making process regarding the future of the business, and they share in profits as well as losses. As with a sole proprietorship, all profits or losses are recorded on the owners' personal tax returns, and the owners must pay self-employment taxes on any earnings. Also similar to a sole proprietorship, a partnership does not require state-level registration.

The remaining corporate structures listed below *do* require registration with your secretary of state.

Limited Liability Company (LLC)

A Limited Liability Company (LLC) is a hybrid structure, in the sense that it combines some of the elements of a sole proprietorship or partnership with some of the features of a corporation (described below). Specifically, an LLC is like a sole proprietorship or general partnership in the sense that it is generally taxed just like those simpler entities, which means that profits are passed through the business to its proprietor(s), and are only taxed at the time they're reported as income. Owners must pay self-employment taxes on any income received from an LLC just as they would in a sole proprietorship or general partnership. At the same time, an LLC is similar to a corporation in the sense that its shareholders enjoy limited liability—meaning, they are only liable up to a fixed amount, usually the level of their own investment. But there's no such thing as stock in an LLC; the only way to add or remove new owners or investors is by amending the company's charter, which typically requires help from a lawyer.

C Corporation

A C corporation is an independent legal entity that is responsible for its own actions and liabilities, while its ownership is dispersed among shareholders. Unlike in an LLC, the profits of a C corporation are effectively taxed twice: first, when they're reported as corporate profit, and second, when they're disbursed to shareholders as dividends. To the extent a shareholder is also an employee of a C corporation, his salary is treated just like any other employee's salary—payroll taxes and all—and is viewed as completely separate from any compensation that may come in the form of dividends. C corporations are generally most attractive for businesses that want to issue stock to investors, often including business investors (like venture capital firms), with different classes of rights and responsibilities for different shareholders.

S Corporation

S corporations are similar to C corporations in the sense that they have wide flexibility in issuing stock, but they're *not* subject to double taxation. Instead, S-corp profits are passed through the business to shareholders in a manner similar to an LLC. Unlike in an LLC, however, the owner(s) of an S corporation need not pay self-employment taxes. Instead, any shareholder who is working for the company must receive "reasonable" wages for that labor, and those wages are then subject to income and payroll taxes. Any profits left over after salaries, however, are *not* subject to payroll taxes. However, in order to reap these tax benefits and maintain

S-corp status, S corporations are subject to certain restrictions that C corporations are not. Principally, S corporations can only issue stock to individuals—not companies—and can only issue a finite number of them. Furthermore, S corporations can only have one "class" of stock—meaning, they can't give different classes of shareholder rights and responsibilities.

A company that has organized as an S corporation can change its status to C corporation relatively easily.

	Sole Proprietor	General Partnership	LLC	C Corp	S Corp
Easily formed by operation of law—no requirement to file anything with state govt.	✓	✓			
Owners receive limited liability protection from certain business debts and obligations			✓	✓	✓
No requirement to hold annual meetings or maintain corporate records	✓	✓	✓		
Tax liability "passes through" organization directly to owners (avoids "double-taxation")	✓	✓	✓		✓
Active owners are treated as employees for purposes of payroll taxes and fringe benefits				✓	✓
Ownership interest is freely transferrable (by issuing, buying, and selling shares of stock)				✓	✓
Business may be perpetual in duration			✓	✓	✓
Can have nonindividual corporate investors (e.g., a venture capital firm)			✓	✓	
May have unlimited owners/ investors, with different classes of rights and responsibilities		✓	✓	✓	

Now that you've got a general sense of the options available to you, we'll go through some questions intended to guide you toward the alternative that makes the most sense for your specific needs.

Which corporate structure, and where, makes sense for *your* business?

Each type of corporate structure has pros and cons. Ask yourself the following questions in order to narrow the options.

1. **Do you have employees?** If not, and if you're planning on operating without any for at least a little while, you can bypass the headache of formally registering your business by starting out as a sole proprietorship (or partnership, if applicable). Forming an LLC, a C corp, or an S corp will afford you certain legal protections that are good to have if you have employees, but the hassle of incorporating might not be worth it if you don't. You can always decide to tackle the issue of corporate formation down the road, when you're ready to grow and hire employees. And in the meantime, you can operate with the simplest possible business structure, and run the business out of your personal bank account and with your own tax ID number.

2. **Are you planning on operating exclusively or primarily in one state?** If your business will be operating mainly in one state, it probably makes sense to do your corporate filing in that state. If not, then you've got options. Due to a friendly tax and legal system in the state of Delaware, that's where the vast majority of tech start-ups choose to incorporate. In fact, **if you're planning on seeking venture capital funding,**

then filing in Delaware is a good idea, simply because that's what most VC firms expect to see. **If you're not going to seek venture capital, and if you're not excited about traveling to a Delaware courthouse in the event that you ever get sued, then simply file where you primarily do business.**

3. **How do you plan on providing benefits to your family?** If you like the idea of using a Professional Employer Organization to outsource all of your company's HR (as I strongly recommend, and described in detail in Chapter Four), that gives you the flexibility to enroll yourself, and your family, into a shared system for healthcare and 401(k) benefits. But that works best if you've classified yourself as an employee of the company you own—and that's really only possible in a corporation, because the owner cannot also be an employee of an LLC, a Sole Proprietorship, or a Partnership.
4. **Do you plan on seeking investment capital from professional investors?** Many venture capitalists and other investors prefer, or even require, the companies they fund to be registered as C corporations. The start-up accelerator program Y Combinator recommends that you use the site Clerky.com to draw up standard incorporation papers that will automatically follow the best practices for start-ups seeking venture capital. In fact, Clerky will organize your business in precisely the way investors expect, to prevent your corporate structure from creating any wrinkles in the funding process.
5. **Will multiple parties have an ownership stake?** There are lots of benefits to forming as an LLC, including practically

limitless flexibility in structuring your company. But in an LLC, everything is done with contracts, and investors can't easily sell their interests in the business; everyone involved is more or less a partner. On top of that, if someone dies, figuring out what happens to their ownership stake isn't as simple as bequeathing shares of stock. So if you need ownership flexibility, forming a corporation may be your best bet. That gives you the ability to issue shares of stock that can easily be sold, bequeathed, traded, etc. On the downside, corporations are required to hold annual meetings and record minutes from those meetings, which isn't required in an LLC. **If your company is likely to experience changes in ownership, then the specific requirements of an LLC actually may be more onerous than those of a corporation.**

6. **How much do you plan on making . . . realistically?** The corporate structure you choose will have a ton of tax implications—far too many to discuss fully in these pages. But, broadly speaking, most small businesses choose *not* to organize as a C corp because of the double-taxation issue discussed above. Both LLCs and S corps are pass-through entities, so profits are only taxed once, when they're declared as individual income. There are other tax distinctions between LLCs and S corporations, however. In an LLC, all earnings are considered partnership income, and are therefore subject to self-employment taxes (that is, the equivalent of both the employer's and employee's share of payroll taxes). In an S corp, however, the owner is considered an employee of the company, not a partner, and must receive

a "reasonable" salary as a W-2 employee, and pay payroll taxes on that salary. But any profits that come into an S corp beyond that salary are *not* subject to payroll taxes, which is a benefit. At the same time, an S corp is actually required to pay unemployment insurance for the owner/employee, even though said owner/employee can never really draw unemployment compensation. Meanwhile, an LLC owner doesn't pay unemployment insurance for him or herself, since in that situation, the owner is not an employee. So, at the end of the day, which one is better? It depends on how your salary compares to company profits. **If most profits will be captured in your salary, an LLC is probably better. If not, then an S corporation is likely the smarter route.**

7. **How big do you hope to grow in the long term?** Sole proprietorships and partnerships often make sense for very small—*micro* small—companies. Once they've grown a bit, most small businesses choose to incorporate as LLCs or S corps, while larger companies typically choose LLC or C corp status. So it's worth thinking about your plan for the long term. It's also quite easy to convert an S corp into a C corp down the road, but it's *not* very easy to convert an LLC to a C corp (just ask Mr. Zuckerberg). Conversely, **if you think the ownership structure of your business will be simple enough that an LLC structure will work for you even as your business grows, then that's often a great option.**

As you can see, there is no one-size-fits-all approach to the question of corporate structure, but hopefully, the above has given you some good food for thought. Before you make a final decision, I recommend bringing a trusted CLO into your C-suite, as discussed in Chapter Four, to help you navigate this important issue.

A Word of Caution: The Limits of Limited Liability

Many entrepreneurs mistakenly believe that forming an LLC or a corporation protects them from getting sued; the phrase "limited liability" seems to suggest as much. But that's a grave mistake.

In particular, the concept of limited liability actually refers to shareholders—that is, your *investors*—as opposed to you as owner, or your employees. In fact, the corporation first came into being as a means of protecting shareholders from becoming personally liable for the debts of the businesses in which they've invested. The corporate structure allowed businesses to access investment capital more easily, because investors were more willing to open their pockets when they were insulated from liability.

But that means that **owners, partners, and employees at LLCs and corporations are still very much liable if they commit unlawful acts**. The two most common types of behavior that lead to personal liability by an employee, member, or shareholder of a corporation or LLC are (1) "piercing the corporate veil," and (2) individual responsibility for torts. "Piercing the corporate veil" means a business owner has failed to uphold the requirements of the corporate structure; most often, that means failing to hold regular board meetings and keeping the requisite minutes, or allowing business funds to comingle with personal funds. Individual responsibility for torts includes breach of fiduciary responsibilities, negligence, fraud, and misrepresentation.

In other words, "limited liability" only gets you so far. If you're on the wrong side of the law, you'll get sued.

But enough about that. Let's turn to the urgent issue of how to fund your new enterprise.

How should I fund my business when I'm starting out?

Without a supply of cold, hard cash, it's hard to get any business off the ground. And as we've discussed, a lack of adequate start-up capital is the number-two reason that new businesses fail. So the question of how to fund your fledgling enterprise is critically important. Here are the most common funding strategies, and the pros and cons of each.

Self-funding (a.k.a. Bootstrapping)

For reasons that will become increasingly clear as we move through the other funding options below, self-funding is *the* answer for the vast majority of businesses when they are first starting out. It's not necessarily the funding method that entrepreneurs *prefer*, but it becomes the default method due to a simple lack of alternatives.

At the same time, bootstrapping—as self-funding is often called—has a number of distinct advantages. I have a few start-ups under my belt, and I've had the experience of bootstrapping *and* the experience of starting businesses with outside funding. **When you're bootstrapping, you can't afford to waste a dime, and that thrift often forces entrepreneurs to slow down and choose wisely; the wisdom "slow is fast" becomes especially relevant.** (And if you remember all the way back to Part I of this book, some of the most important start-up capital that entrepreneurs put on the line is their own time. In a bootstrap scenario, it's absolutely crucial to allocate your time wisely.)

Meanwhile, when you're playing with someone else's money, it's easy to move fast—way too fast. You can get into a lot of trouble moving quickly in the wrong direction before you've clarified the core of your business model and adequately tested the core hypotheses on your Business Model Canvas.

A separate advantage of bootstrapping—and one that can prove extraordinarily valuable down the road—is the fact that you don't have to give up any equity or control in your business. If you take money from a venture capitalist or angel investor, as described below, it always comes with some serious strings attached. But **when you're self-funding, the business is yours and yours alone.**

Of course, the stress and penny-pinching that go along with bootstrapping have brought plenty of small-business owners to their wits' end. Self-funding brings a number of advantages, but comfort and luxury sure aren't among them.

Friends and Family

The next most common funding method is usually a supplement to the first. Entrepreneurs often go to their friends and family to supplement whatever they can scrape together on their own. After all, the people closest to you, who know and trust you more than anyone else, are the most likely to believe in your vision and have faith in your ability to execute it.

The obvious downside, of course, is the age-old wisdom that you should never lend money to your friends and family. Borrowing from those closest to you has the potential to spoil those relationships, especially if everything doesn't go as planned (but sometimes even when things *do* go as planned, or even *better* than planned).

There are lots of ways to mitigate this downside risk. In fact, I think entrepreneurs often aren't creative enough when it comes to structuring a loan from family or friends. You can opt to make the loan a high-interest convertible note. You can also offer equity in the business by devising dynamic equity splits that take into account the value of their contribution.

But regardless of how you structure this type of loan, don't skimp on the contracts. Yes, that's right: **You've *got* to have contracts, drafted by a lawyer, even with—maybe even *especially* with—your family and friends.** Whether things go very well in the future of your business, or very poorly, you'll need extremely clear and detailed contracts. As emphasized in Chapter Four, your CLO is an essential team member. A CLO specializes in managing relationships and expectations with all key stakeholders, including family investors. You need a professional who will literally get everyone's expectations, for the short term and long term, on the same page from day one. This is *especially* true when the relationships are as dear as close friends and family.

Crowdfunding

This is a relatively new source of capital for start-ups, made legal in 2012 through federal legislation commonly referred to as the JOBS Act. While not for everyone, crowdfunding can be a great way to get a product-driven business off the ground.

How does it work? In essence, you use a crowdfunding site like Kickstarter or Indiegogo as a portal through which supporters can donate to your start-up funds. To attract as many funders as possible, businesses typically offer incentives, and they tend to offer bigger and bigger incentives for larger donations (such incentives range from T-shirts to getting the new product for free when it launches). Often, the campaign functions as a platform for supporters to preorder the product even before it actually exists. According to market research conducted by the domain company Panabee, crowdfunding works best for products related to technology, gaming, and design.

On the downside, you'll lose about 5 percent of any money you raise to the crowdsourcing website that hosts your campaign, and then, often, more money to credit-card processing and other fees. That will chip away at the funds you raise.

On the upside, **crowdfunding can be a great way to test demand for your product before you've invested too much capital in building it. And sometimes the capital raised through crowdfunding is sufficient for building the minimum viable product (MVP)—and thus, all of a sudden, you have the funding, product, and momentum you need in order to launch.**

Crowdfunding can also function as part of a broader marketing campaign. For that reason, it's best if you're drawing on the expertise of an outsourced CMO to design and launch your campaign as part of an initial marketing strategy. You're shooting for a powerful campaign that will establish a community of cheerleaders for your product and thus, a relatively strong preliminary customer base.

Small-Business Grants

If free money sounds too good to be true, well, that's because it is. The application process for small-business grants tends to be quite tedious, with no guarantee of success; given the value of your time, a small-business grant definitely isn't free. Nonetheless, it's a funding source that's available to select start-ups, even as most entrepreneurs never consider the possibility.

So if your business is building something that the federal government might consider a public good—something in the fields of education, medicine, and even certain kinds of technology—it may be worth the effort to run a quick search through Grants.gov. You might find a funding source that's well suited to your business.

Small-Business Loans

This option often sounds attractive at the outset, but often becomes less so as entrepreneurs learn the banks' requirements. In particular, banks are in the business of making *low-risk* loans, and there's nothing low-risk about a business that has zero sales history. Thus, banks generally only make small-business loans that are backed by valuable collateral, which means that unless you have great credit and significant resources to use as collateral, or substantial equity in your home that you're willing to put on the line for your new business, bank loans are difficult to get.

But difficult doesn't mean impossible, and if you can get a bank loan, you'll enjoy the relatively low interest rates.

If you do decide to pursue this funding route, make sure you're specifically seeking a Small Business Administration (SBA) Loan. The SBA has special programs designed to help launch small businesses, and represents a far better option than other types of loans.

There are also a variety of businesses and consultants that specialize in helping start-ups access funding from banks and credit unions. They'll know the universe of options available to you, and they'll understand how to leverage any specific features of your business. And if no bank funding is available, they may also be able to match you with a loan from a nontraditional lending institution. That would come with a higher interest rate, but it might be worth it.

Venture Capital and Angel Investors

You've heard the wisdom that great risk can bring great reward. You've also heard its corollary: low risk offers little reward. Your local bank makes loans that fall in the latter category: low risk, with modest earnings. Meanwhile, venture capitalists take on a lot of risk seeking great reward.

Specifically, angel investors and venture capitalists bet on early-stage companies (often referred to as "seed stage" companies) in exchange for what they hope will be a big payday. This business model presupposes that most of these seed start-ups will fail, but that the ones that succeed will deliver such wildly high returns that, on balance, it's more profitable than putting the same money in the stock market instead.

This funding source is unavailable to the vast majority of start-ups because such investors are only interested in companies that have the potential to bring in *astronomical* returns. They're looking for something that's scalable and could be the next Facebook. That means a local coffee shop—even if successful by local coffee shop standards—will never make the cut. The types of companies that *can* access this sort of funding tend to be tech start-ups or other companies that are completely product-driven, or have a similarly scalable and high-potential model.

Yet even if your business *is* in a position to attract this type of funding, there are plenty of reasons to think twice before pursuing it. **Venture capital and angel investments are by far the riskiest**

funding source an entrepreneur can have—again, the opposite of a bank loan. Yes, **such investors might give you tons of money when a bank never would, and that's seductive, but it will cost you.**

In exchange for taking such a big risk, investors take equity in your company and often a seat (or multiple seats) on your board. That trade might not bother you, since those things only become valuable if you're wildly successful, and at that point, you're rich anyway. But you can get burned; these investors care about their investment, not you. When a company becomes successful, it's not uncommon for investors to use their power on the board to fire the founding CEO and replace him with someone more seasoned, since the skill set necessary for running a big company is very different from that of founding a start-up. In other words, **you could find yourself fired from the company you built.**

Still interested? Here's some basic background on venture capital.

First off, what's the different between angel investors and venture capitalists? Increasingly, the line between them is blurred. But broadly speaking, the venture capital field consists of firms specializing in specific industries that make large investments in companies that have at least an initial track record of success. That is, they're looking for businesses that have already proven their product-market fit and the scalability of their business model. On the other hand, angel investors tend to be individuals—often former entrepreneurs—who are willing to make investments of varying size in companies that have no track record at all.

Accessing funding from either a VC or an angel investor is very, very difficult; the odds are against you. If you do choose to pursue this route, there are a couple potential paths.

The first is to start by self-funding, perhaps supplemented with capital from friends and family. You bootstrap long enough to prove product-market fit, or at least to sufficiently establish the right side of your Business Model Canvas. Then you go after an angel investor. Subsequently, you use that angel capital to prove the scalability of your business model in order to then attract a "Series A" round of funding from a venture capital firm.

Alternatively, you could pursue an accelerator program like the one offered by the seed funder Y Combinator. That program accepts a few dozen businesses at a time, and then Y Combinator actually provides those entrepreneurs with a living stipend in addition to a crash course of best practices delivered by highly successful entrepreneurs. Then, once you've "graduated" from Y Combinator, doors in the venture capital world suddenly open to you. Sound great? First, you have to get admitted. The winning applicants tend to have a strong team of founders—often with a pedigree education from somewhere like Stanford—and/or a strong track record of successful start-ups under their belt, *plus* an amazing idea that could potentially be worth many millions (if not billions).

Any way you slice it, venture capital and angel investments are a dangerous, complicated, and expensive means of securing funding for your business. But for a select few, it's the right way to go.

Form, Fund, and Grow

Of course, the purpose of establishing your corporate structure and getting hold of start-up capital is to put your business in the position to finally *grow*. And that means attracting customers, keeping them, and expanding your customer base. And how do you do *that?* You'll find out in the next chapter.

15

Grow: Questions about Sales and Marketing

I've learned that people will forget what you said, people will forget what you did, but people will never forget how you made them feel.

—Maya Angelou
(American Poet, 1928–2014)

Whether you're just launching your business or you've been in business for years, some of your most pressing concerns are probably about attracting customers and growing your revenue. So this chapter addresses these fundamental questions:

1. **How do I get customers?**
2. **What's the right marketing budget?**
3. **How do I keep customers?**
4. **How do I grow my revenue?**

We'll answer each of these questions in turn. But before we can properly identify the right strategies for attracting customers and growing your revenue, we've first got to identify the *wrong* strategies because it's easy to get distracted by flashy marketing tactics that often turn out to be a waste of time and money.

Throughout this book, we've talked about how the entrepreneurial itch can lead new business owners to act quickly and to skip the development stage that's necessary for launching a successful business. In fact, many entrepreneurs don't bother refining their business model in order to establish great product-market fit. Oftentimes, they omit that crucial work and jump straight to the questions above, imagining that marketing is the only thing standing between them and a wildly successful company.

It would be fantastic if that were true. But I'm afraid that marketing alone—that is, great branding, or a great website, or a great e-mail strategy, or packaging, or signage—is almost *never* the whole answer to any of the questions above. Why?

Because once you've done the work of understanding *exactly* who your customers are and *exactly* what they want, and then mapping out *precisely* how your business model solves a need or a want that's keeping them up at night—well, by that point, you're about 88 percent of the way to a marketing strategy that will blow your competition out of the water. And how to accomplish that last 12 percent often becomes pretty clear.

Think back for a second to Sue and her bagel shop. Had Sue moved forward with her initial bagel shop idea without first testing her assumptions, she would have invested in a physical storefront as the centerpiece of her branding and marketing plan. She would have put out great signage; she would have advertised deals for getting a free bagel with the purchase of a dozen; she would have offered special breakfast sandwiches as well as goodies like freshly squeezed OJ and smoked salmon.

But the best marketing strategies in the world wouldn't have turned that bagel shop into a success, because Sue was trying to solve a nonexistent problem. Sue's potential customers didn't care about quality bagels, and brilliant marketing just can't salvage a company that lacks product-market fit. Luckily, Sue didn't make that mistake; instead, she tested her assumptions. And by the end of her testing phase, she had an entirely different business model. It even had a different name: "Sue's Bagels" had morphed into "Sue's Sweets." Good thing she didn't spend a lot of money branding "Sue's Bagels" on day one.

Yet most entrepreneurs do exactly that, because it's damn temping to jump right into designing a logo and printing business cards and renting office space before taking the time to check if anyone actually cares. Unfortunately, a year down the road, these very same entrepreneurs begin to wonder why revenue is so stubbornly low.

That's why **your first and best strategy for attracting customers and growing your revenue is to be 100 percent certain—through lots of diligent testing—that your value proposition truly serves your target customer. By making that your first order of business, you'll put yourself far ahead of most of your competition.**

OK, you've done that. You're sure? Good. You're on your way to success. Now let's turn to customer relationships.

How Do I Get Customers?

The Business Model Canvas makes the significance of Customer Relationships exceedingly clear. Take a quick look and notice how Customer Relationships is one of only two connectors between your Value Proposition and your Customer Segments.

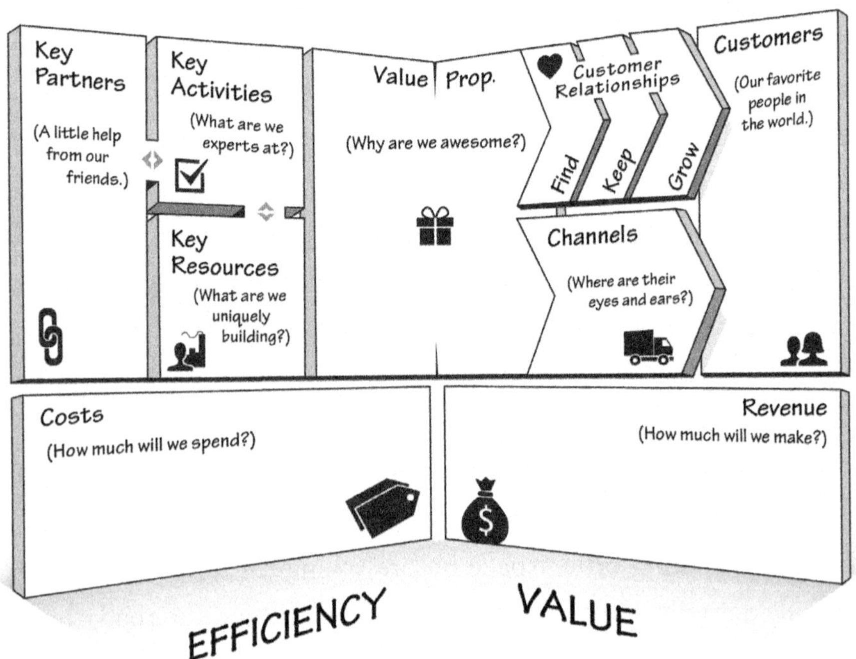

Your Value Proposition, of course, is the reason your business exists. More precisely, your business exists to deliver that specific value to your specific customer base. And how do you do that? You've got to have a viable distribution method, naturally, which is captured on your canvas as Channels. But even more importantly, you've got to establish a relationship with those customers; otherwise, they'll never know you exist, and they'll never give your value proposition a chance. And that means **you can't have product-market fit without customer relationships**. It's no less important than that.

Back to Sue and her bagels. With some market research, Sue quickly learned that her storefront idea was bunk, because her target customers valued convenience more than anything. Lightbulb! Sue brought her bagels directly to those customers, because nothing could be more convenient than that. Imagine that you're one of Sue's potential customers. You're in too much of a hurry in the morning to have breakfast (sound familiar?), so by ten a.m., you're ravenous. You walk by the break room and—*what?*—there's a spread of freshly baked bagels. You're *thrilled.*

The poet Maya Angelou once said, "I've learned that people will forget what you said, people will forget what you did, but people will never forget how you made them feel." Well, Sue made her customers *happy*—surprised, and happy. Thus, those customers connected with her business in a powerful way. You can't do much better than that, although then Sue actually *did* do better than that. She went on to partner with Feeding America to give her customers not only blissful convenience, but also the self-satisfaction of contributing to a cause that mattered to them. Sue's brand was now linked to a whole lot of good feeling.

> People don't buy what you do; they buy why you do it. And what you do simply proves what you believe.
>
> —Simon Sinek (British Writer)

This isn't unique to Sue's story. Smart companies in every industry position their brands to connect with their key customer segments on an emotional level. Yours must too; that's the beginning of a successful **branding strategy.**

Building strong customer relationships requires a branding strategy that connects your business to your customers on a powerful emotional level. To achieve that, you've got to know your customers inside and out, and you've got to offer a value proposition that relates to their specific needs/wants *and* emotions.

As author Simon Sinek said, "People don't buy what you do; they buy why you do it. And what you do simply proves what you believe." So ask yourself, *why am I doing what I do? What do I believe?*

More specifically, what inspired you to start your business in the first place? What are you so unrelenting passionate about that you've been willing to make all the sacrifices you've made in order to get your business off the ground? The more you allow your customers to feel and connect with that passion, the more attracted to your company they'll be.

At the same time, potential customers will generally only give you a second—or a fraction of a second—to demonstrate that passion and value. But that's OK, because by this stage of the process, you've boiled down your core value proposition to its simplest, clearest terms. In other words, **your focused, refined value proposition, communicated with the same passion that led you to start your business in the first place, should form the basis of your branding strategy and your subsequent marketing efforts**.

Once you're clear about both your value and passion, it's time to get into the specifics of how to **amplify** your brand in order to attract customers. That is, how will you get your business in front of the eyeballs of your target customers?

Let's turn to some tactics.

Just as was the case with corporate formation in the last chapter, there's no one-size-fits-all approach to marketing. But there are some key pieces of wisdom that are relevant no matter your industry or business model. And the first one is that **the best marketing doesn't feel like marketing**.

Think about the difference between placing a banner of your company name at a local community event versus volunteering at that event. The first tactic is clearly marketing, while the second one is more of a contribution to the community. And the second one is the one that's more likely to actually bring in customers because, through volunteering at the event, you'll have important conversations and develop new connections. It might not feel like marketing while you're doing it, but it's the better strategy by far.

Or think back to the story of Dropbox in Chapter Seven. The founders put out a video for their target audience, and that video was chockablock full of hilarious inside jokes that the audience—and, as a matter of fact, the founders, themselves—loved. It might not have felt like marketing, but it was one of the shrewdest strategies ever to emerge from a tech start-up.

Then there's the small-town pizza shop that I talked about in Chapter Twelve, where there's a chalkboard on which customers log their recent wildlife sightings. The owners of that pizza shop weren't trying to devise a cunning marketing ploy with that chalkboard, yet it turned out to offer valuable social connection for community members, thereby fostering loyalty to their pizza shop.

All of these examples underscore the fact that **good marketing creates value for the customer segments *without* a direct focus on bringing in revenue**. The best marketing is more like a gift to your customers; essentially, it's value that they don't directly pay for. On the Business Model Canvas, Customer Relationships are separate from Revenue Streams, reflecting the idea that you create different kinds of value for your customers: the value they pay for, which goes under Revenue Streams, and the value they *don't* pay for, which goes under Customer Relationships.

Hopefully, this notion that the best marketing doesn't feel like marketing has already given you some ideas. What's the equivalent of that funny Dropbox video for your business? How about that chalkboard with wildlife sightings?

Now let's get one step more specific, because **the right kind of marketing depends on what type of business you have.** Do you have a storefront? A Web business? A product that gets sold on the shelves of retail outlets like Walmart? Depending on the answer, you'll employ very different marketing tactics.

- If your business has a **physical storefront** or is a **restaurant**, then the location, signage, and décor are critical components of your branding strategy, and the goal is to convince people to walk through your door.

- For a **Web business**, enticing prospective customers to visit your website is your goal. Most likely, that means building a robust social media and content marketing strategy, coupled with a targeted AdWords campaign and smart promotion through partner sites and free media. Then the quality, style, and voice of your site are the chief ambassador for your brand, and it's the variable that will guide customers' purchasing decisions. Meanwhile, the physical office space in which you actually work adds no direct value to your customers, and matters only in terms of the productivity and happiness of your team.
- For a **consumer product** that you're trying to sell through retail outlets, your brand is your packaging, and your marketing efforts are dedicated to introducing that packaging to your target customer, creating a positive association, and ultimately convincing them to take the leap of selecting your product amid a sea of competition.
- For **services** such as those provided by a lawyer or an accountant, there may be no more powerful branding tool than a simple business card and some quality letterhead, while the best marketing may be through networking and community events.

Regardless of which tactics are right for your business model, and which are most natural for you and your team, **the key to a successful marketing strategy is to test, test, test. Every new customer is an experiment; collecting and reviewing the data from each such experiment is an important way of listening to your customers.**

Sometimes that means actually *listening* to your customers, by asking them questions in person or through a survey tool. The answers they give you—like the answers Sue got simply by talking to customers at existing bagel shops—are known in economics lingo as "stated preferences." Those are the preferences that your customers are willing and able to articulate. That's valuable information.

But there's an even more valuable type of information to be had. You've heard the expression that actions speak louder than words. Well, it's important to listen to what your customers tell you, but it's even more important to observe what they actually *do*—or, in economics parlance, to observe their "revealed preferences." Do people continually tell you that your new product is great, but decline to buy it? Prospective customers repeatedly told Sue that her bagels were delicious, but their purchasing behavior suggested that convenience was all that really mattered.

In other words, **the best marketing (1) focuses first and foremost on developing the tightest possible product-market fit; (2) fosters a powerful emotional connection between the customer segments and the brand; (3) implements marketing tactics that are tailored to the specific business model; and (4) tests, tests, and tests again, in order to develop the most effective strategy for attracting and serving your target market.**

What's the Right Marketing Budget?

The answer to this question is both very simple and extremely complicated. The simple answer is that **you should keep growing your marketing budget as long as it delivers a positive ROI; if you bring in $1.01 for every $1 you spend on marketing, then keep**

growing that budget. After all, trading $1 for $1.01 is like having a money-printing machine.

The complexity, however, comes in figuring out whether your marketing efforts are actually making money or not. They key term we use at Agents of Efficiency in order to answer this question is the **Lifetime Value (LTV)** of a customer. After factoring in all the costs associated with providing your product or service to a customer throughout the average duration of a customer relationship, how much profit will you make? That number is your LTV.

The other relevant term is your **Customer Acquisition Cost (CAC)**. That is, after accounting for the costs of your marketing efforts plus properly valuing the time it took you and/or team members to implement those efforts, how much does it cost your business, on average, to bring in a new customer?

Caution! Don't try this at home! I'm guessing that the prospect of calculating your LTV and your CAC is pretty intimidating. Don't worry. There's a reason you've got that outsourced expert CFO in your C-suite. Few, if any, CEOs—whether at the helm of very large businesses or very small ones—can or should attempt to calculate LTVs and CACs on their own. This is a place where financial expertise is all but required.

Once you've figured out your LTV and your CAC, the formula is pretty simple:

If CAC < LTV, then ☺

In other words, **as long as your CAC is less than your LTV, you should keep growing your marketing budget, and growing it some more, because you're virtually printing money.** Here's a quick example of what that looks like in practice.

Let's say I run a law firm in which my clients are businesses. I calculate that a typical small-business client will pay my firm about $5,000 per year, and it costs my firm a total of about $4,000 to actually provide legal counsel annually for that client. That puts my profit margin at about $1,000 per year per client. Then, let's further assume that my average client relationship lasts 4.5 years. That means that the LTV of an average customer is $4,500.

Now, what am I willing to spend in order to bring a new client into my firm? I'm willing to spend anything *up to* $4,499. In other words, I can sustain a CAC of up to $4,499 and still turn a profit.

If you're like most people, you read that last paragraph and you're now saying to yourself, "Only *one measly dollar* in profit for all that work over the lifetime of a customer? That's not *nearly* enough!" Hold on; let me explain.

Think for a second about how we calculated profit margin. We said that a typical client will pay about $5,000 a year, and that all the costs and overhead associated with doing the work for that client amount to $4,000, yielding a profit of $1,000. Now consider the fact the $4,000 in costs includes *every single relevant expense*, from a market-rate salary for me, the attorney and owner of the firm, all the way to electricity and paper for the copy machines. So the $1,000 in profit is *truly* profit; it's the revenue over and above every associated cost, including a healthy salary for the CEO.

Now let's go back to the question of the marketing budget. Given an LTV of $4,500—in which every penny of that $4,500 represents pure profit—how much is the owner of this firm willing to spend on marketing? Any amount up to $4,499. As soon as the CAC hits $4,500, the firm will just break even, and for anything more than $4,500, it will lose money.

Now back to determining your marketing budget. You're probably beginning to see why coming up with the right budget is both really simple and really complicated. "CAC < LTV, then ☺" is straightforward, but accurately determining your precise CAC and LTV is much more difficult. You've got to have a CFO in your corner, because it's easy to underestimate your CAC and to overestimate your LTV—and, subsequently, to spend more acquiring new customers than those customers are actually worth to your business.

So **when you're just getting started, the best approach is to tread lightly and prioritize.** *Tread lightly* means admitting that you don't yet know your precise LTV or CAC, and that you're basically doing guesswork. Just to be safe, avoid any marketing investments that might push your CAC too close to your LTV, and do so by prioritizing. There are a million potential marketing tactics available to you. In fact, there are so many that the choice can be overwhelming. Start with the low-hanging fruit; choose the tactics that will bring in new customers at the lowest cost. *Then* begin to work your way up the tree.

Giant corporations like Apple, Microsoft, and Coca-Cola probably employ marketing tactics that push their CACs right up against the upper-limit of their LTVs. Why? Because they've already gotten all the low-hanging fruit, and because they have billions of dollars in their coffers, so they can push their marketing budgets to the upper boundary, and even sometimes *exceed* that boundary as part of a learning process to understand which strategies work and which don't.

But you don't have billions of dollars at your disposal, and you haven't yet exhausted every affordable tactic for bringing in new customers. Consider that law firm example, and the fact that there are probably a lot of different ways that firm could spend $4,499 to acquire a new customer. But there are also plenty of strategies that could probably bring in new customers at a cost of, say, $1,000 a piece. Clearly, the firm should exhaust all of those less expensive strategies before moving to more costly ones.

And ideally, your CFO isn't your only C-suite teammate helping you in this process; you also want a Chief Marketing Officer. Though a CMO is typically the final addition to a small-business C-suite, having the know-how and passion of someone who lives and breathes marketing is a game-changer. From choosing which tactics to try first to tweaking, improving, and hopefully reducing your CAC over time, a CMO can provide invaluable leadership.

How Do I Keep Customers?

Contrary to popular belief, the magic formula for keeping customers *isn't* simply great customer service. Let me say that again. **By itself, great customer service isn't enough to keep your customers happy and loyal.** I'm not saying customer service doesn't matter. It does; it's very important. What's more, as a small business, you have the ability to provide great customer service *paired with* social connection in a way that larger companies just can't, as discussed in detail in Chapter Twelve. Those things can add real value to your customers and—*if done right*—your customers will be willing to pay for it.

But what does *done right* mean? Well, if your customer is choosing between your product and an equivalent product sold by a competitor, and you offer better customer service—and/or social value on top of the product itself—then customers will choose your product every time. After all, if that's the only difference between your product and that of your competitor's, why *wouldn't* they choose you? But while customer service may motivate consumer loyalty when all else is equal, customers will very rarely tolerate an inferior product in exchange for better service. And while they may be willing to pay a bit more for an equivalent product delivered with great service *plus* local social connection, they probably won't pay *astronomically* more.

In other words, customer service is no silver bullet. In fact, Forbes has reported some surprising numbers to indicate that customer service may not be the driver of customer retention—and, thus, profitability—at all. According to data on publicly traded companies, the most hated companies in the US actually outperform their well-liked peers, as measured by stock market returns.[20] That means that strong customer service doesn't guarantee profitability, and that sometimes, those two things don't even go together. Of course, the data reported in Forbes are for large corporations, and you're running a small business, but there's an important lesson here for businesses of all sizes: **The key to retaining customers *isn't* customer service; it's brilliant execution of your business model.**

Here are a couple of real-life examples. Recently, I needed to hire a Web designer for my website. What drove my final decision? It was pretty simple, actually: (1) price, and (2) the anticipated quality of the finished website. After all, this website will be around for years, and it's a critical part of my company's brand. In that equation, how much did customer service matter? Not a whole heck of a lot. I don't really care if the developer provides incredible customer service, or even if he goes above and beyond and takes my family out to dinner during the development phase. If the end result is a $15,000 website that is no better (or worse) than what someone else could have knocked out for $1,500 using Squarespace, then I want the cheaper option, because $13,500 is one expensive dinner.

But consider the small-town pizza shop from Chapter Twelve. In that case, social connection is part of the core value proposition—and, at the same time, the shop sells delicious pizza at reasonable prices. If the pizza weren't good, or the price was too high, the chalkboard with wildlife sightings and the larger feeling of social connection probably wouldn't be enough to protect that shop from being gobbled up by a competitor.

Back to our initial question: How do I keep customers?

The answer is to **be the best at what you do. Learn everything you can about who your customers are and what makes them tick. What are their wants, needs, and pain points? Obsess about how to solve those pain points for them and how to help them achieve those wants, and how to do it better all the time. Your customers will stay because they couldn't bear to leave.**

And you'll see the difference in your bottom line. Research by Bain Capital suggests that improving your rate of customer retention by just 5 percent can translate to an increase in profitability of 25 to 95 percent.[21] Wow! Enough said.

How Do I Grow My Revenue?

We've already covered the questions of attracting customers and keeping them—both of which, of course, translate into revenue growth. A third approach to raising revenue is to bring in more money through your existing customer base. Think back to your LTV and CAC. Remember that your LTV is the total lifetime value of a customer, and your CAC is how much it costs you to acquire that customer. Well, the difference between them is your profit:

LTV – CAC = Profit

So while you can increase profit by going out and getting new customers, another approach is simply to raise your LTV (or decrease your CAC, which your COO and CFO work on together).

It's easy to underestimate the potential in raising your LTV. Perhaps you think you're already tapping your existing customers for as much as they're willing to spend. But you may very well be wrong about that and the prospective gains may be greater than you can presently imagine.

A couple of statistics bear this out. According to Forbes, 70 percent of repeat customers are willing to consider new products from a company they already trust, and repeat customers spend between 33 percent and 67 percent more than new customers.[22, 23] Meanwhile, depending on your industry and which particular study you're looking at, it costs *five to twenty-five times more* to attract a new customer than to retain an existing customer.[24]

Those stats underscore the potential in your existing customer base. Or to put it in terms of your LTV, **the longer your existing customers remain loyal to you and the more products and services you can sell them, the higher the LTV. And the higher the LTV, the greater the profits.**

So instead of focusing on marketing strategies for bringing in new customers, consider what it would take to increase the duration of your average customer relationship by six months.

How could you improve your value proposition in order to entice your customers to stay with you six months more, on average, than they're currently doing? How much would it cost? Then go to the numbers. If you add six months to your average customer relationship, how much will your LTV increase, and what's the corresponding growth in profits across your entire customer base?

Now consider investing that same sum of money into attracting new customers. What's the potential payoff? Very often, investing in your existing customer base promises a greater return—and sometimes much, *much* greater.

At this point, you might be saying to yourself, *fine, that's all well and good, but how do I actually go about increasing my LTV?* Well, you have options:

- **Improve your existing product(s)** in such a way that will entice your customers to stay with you longer than they do now; or,
- **Add new products, services, or features to your current offerings** in order to increase your revenue flow from your present customer base; or,
- **Do both.**

And how should you go about devising strategies for one or all of the above? You guessed it: experiment.

A great benefit of focusing on your existing customers rather than new customers is that it tends to be quicker and easier to test their preferences. After all, you know *exactly* who your existing customers are, and you have continual contact with them. That's a big opportunity. So go ahead and **set up experiments. Create a continuous feedback loop. Relentlessly explore new ways of**

updating and improving your value proposition to serve your existing customer base in ever more innovative ways.

For a Web business, this might mean A/B testing. For a storefront, perhaps it means changing where and how you place merchandise, signs, and price tags, then watching how your customers respond. For a consumer product, it might mean testing out new packages and labels.

> It's really hard to design products by focus groups. A lot of times, people don't know what they want until you show it to them.
>
> —Steve Jobs (Founder, Apple, 1955–2011)

This is another situation in which the difference between "revealed" preferences and "stated" preferences really matters. Remember what we said about customer service earlier in this chapter: Everyone says it's the most important thing, but actual behavior suggests otherwise. Look for ways not only to collect direct feedback from customers, but also to capture their *actions* in a way that will inform your business model going forward.

But whatever type of data you can get your hands on, **your goal is a continuous process of improving your core value proposition.**

A Good Problem to Have

When a business becomes successful, the flood of customer demands can sometimes dilute the quality of the core product or service, and the virtuous cycle of continuous improvement starts to reverse.

That's why this book ends where it started. **In the final chapter, we'll cover questions about time management, and a new way of looking at the fundamental truth that, while money matters, it's *time* that drives your bottom line.**

16

Flourish: Questions about Time Management and Work–Life Balance

Most of us spend too much time on what is urgent and not enough time on what is important.

—Stephen Covey
(American Writer, 1932–2012)

You can always earn more money, but you can never earn more time. Your time is your ultimate nonrenewable resource, and **whether your goal is to grow your company into the next Facebook or to spend every possible minute with your family, your skill at time management will drive your ability to succeed.**

Meanwhile, the demands on your schedule will likely grow exponentially as your business expands. It's common for a small-business owner to feel crushed beneath the flood of new customers and the ever-increasing workload necessary for keeping the operation afloat. It becomes difficult or impossible for the entrepreneur to enjoy her own success. And that pressure in turn endangers the survival of the business, as its value proposition suffers when the team struggles to serve all the customers knocking at the door.

And that's why ***"How can I manage my time better?"*** **is a question I hear from small-business owners all the time. It's a topic of urgent importance to the survival of your business and to your own happiness. This chapter will help you clarify your goals and develop a new approach to the way you manage your time, so that you're using every possible minute to move the ball forward on whichever priorities are most important to you.**

But often when I start to delve into the details with entrepreneurs who are struggling with time management, I discover that they're actually asking a slightly different question from simply how to better manage their time. It turns out, they're asking something more along the lines of, "*Assuming I continue doing everything I'm doing right now, how can I accomplish more in each day?*"

And here's where this chapter takes a turn from the prevailing wisdom. **You're making an enormous assumption in thinking that you should continue doing all the things you're currently doing, and it's probably not an assumption that serves your best interests.**

> Nothing is less productive than to make more efficient what should not be done at all.
>
> —Peter Drucker (Austrian Writer, 1909–2005)

Let's say you had a way of earning $10,000 per hour any time you wanted. Would you spend your time differently?

Of course you would. You'd spend at least some of your time doing that $10,000-an-hour work. Maybe you wouldn't spend forty hours a week on it—although maybe you would. But I'd venture to guess that something would shift; you would rearrange your schedule to do some of that highly profitable work and, I'm guessing, to make time for some other priorities in your life now that you have the freedom to make more money in less time.

The point is that there's probably room for improvement in your current schedule, even without the opportunity to make $10,000 an hour—though by implementing many of the strategies in this chapter and this book, you're likely to raise your hourly rate considerably higher than its current level.

So, **let's take a hard look at time management, and how to do it better. Then we'll move on to the ever-elusive question of work–life balance.**

How Can I Manage My Time Better?

Instead of a college career filled with parties and copious amounts of beer, I had the distinct pleasure of attending a federal military academy. Requirements like shining my shoes and participating in drills ate up fifteen or even twenty hours every week. I also had a full load of courses, sports, debate team (yes, I was that kind of nerd), and a job as an EMT. I almost went crazy. Then I came up with a strategy, and I've continued to use that same strategy as an adult. In fact, it's been a lifeline for me as an entrepreneur.

It's called **Focus + Lego-based Day Construction.**

The first part—**focus**—might sound obvious; *of course* you should focus on what you're doing. But ask yourself, how often do you try to multitask?

There's a lot of research out there to suggest that multitasking is a myth. Your brain chemistry is such that you actually *can't* concentrate on two things at once. Instead, what you're doing is concentrating on one thing and then toggling over to another, rapidly going back and forth between them. If you're driving and eating, you're ever so briefly taking your concentration off the road in order to take a bite, then immediately, you return to focusing on the road.

You might hate me for saying this, since multitasking is a beloved strategy for many, but, in reality, **when you're multitasking, you're really *not* doing more than one task at once; you're switching quickly between various tasks and doing mediocre work at each one. I'm sorry to be the bearer of bad news, but it's true.**

Remember our friend LeBron? Imagine for a second that when LeBron shows up for practice he actually spends about 10 percent of his time talking on the phone, 10 percent replying to e-mail, and 10 percent on Facebook, all the while practicing drills and shooting free throws in between. Sound like the formula for becoming the greatest basketball talent in the NBA? Not so much.

The same wisdom applies to you. If you truly focus your time and energy on doing *one thing well* in short bursts of time, it will actually allow you to accomplish more work of a greater quality in less time.

Quick Tip: Dealing with Distractions

The problem with focus is that it's often a lot easier said than done. E-mail messages arrive in your inbox, notifications appear on your phone, and ideas pop into your head.

Well, you can turn off the notifications on your phone, and you can choose to look at e-mail only during specific periods of your day that you've scheduled specifically for that task. But what about those great ideas you can't seem to get out of your head?

Write them down.

By writing them down, you'l rest easy knowing that your stroke of genius won't be lost forever, and then you can get back to focusing on the task at hand.

And that brings us to the question of *what.* **What exactly should you accomplish in the few precious hours of each day?**

Try to approach this question with a completely open mind. Rather than thinking about all the things you're doing right now and then removing the ones that don't belong, start with a blank page and consider which tasks truly merit your time. Just because someone asks you to do something doesn't mean you should do it; just because someone asks for an appointment with you doesn't mean you should schedule one. Instead, consider the idea that **your schedule should contain only red-letter, top-priority activities: meetings and appointments that are truly essential; tasks that have to be completed by you and no one else; time for life priorities like being with your spouse and children; and time enough for the unforeseen demands that arise each day.**

Then, once you've got your list of the activities that *truly* merit your time, apply the concept of **Lego-based Day Construction.** Think about your day like you're building something from Legos. What are the fundamental pieces? Then, which are the small pieces that can fit between the big ones? Which are the low-priority pieces—the last ones in and the first ones discarded if necessary?

One of the benefits of thinking about your day in this way is that you'll gain a better understanding of where your time is going. Dropping off a check at the bank, for instance, sounds quick and simple enough. But if you do the math—if you add up the time it takes to drive to the bank, wait in line, and drive home—you start to see the real cost of that activity: Dropping off that check kept you from doing something else. And while *anyone* can drop off a check, there are plenty of tasks that *only you* can do: growing your business, for instance, or spending time with your kids. Suddenly you're considering alternatives: mobile banking? Delegate? (Of course, much of this book has been devoted to strategies for how you, the small-business CEO, can move tasks off of your plate, and we're going to review those strategies in a moment, when we talk about work–life balance.)

In this way, Lego-based Day Construction will help you see where your time is going and then work out how to manage it better. And as you get used to laying out the Lego pieces of each day, you'll get smarter about how much you can accomplish and which tasks actually deserve your time.

Quick Tip: The Efficiency of Synergy

As you're planning each day, try to find related work and batch similar tasks together, because different activities require different types of thinking.

By batching similar activities together, you'll allow your mind to stay "in the zone" instead of forcing yourself to shift gears. Do you need to make a bunch of calls today, or go through a lot of e-mail? Schedule time to make all your calls at once, and respond to all your e-mail at once, instead of allowing them to be diversions throughout the day. You'll also find yourself uncovering all sorts of little hacks and efficiencies to blow through those related tasks faster than you've ever done before.

But maybe the Lego-based approach sounds like too much of your valuable time will be spent on planning; maybe you're asking yourself: **"Am I *really* going to sit there with a blank page and fit the pieces of my day together like a Lego castle?"**

I hear you loud and clear. As a business owner, you know which activities add value for your customers, and which don't. Sitting down with your calendar each day adds no direct value to your customer. But take a second to consider the alternative.

Imagine that you ran your business without a budget. You just spend money willy-nilly. You never keep track of how much comes in or how much goes out. Besides being a tax disaster, that's pretty much a guarantee that your business will go bankrupt. So while no one wants to put together a budget (expect your passionate CFO, of course), it's well worth the time it takes to do so—because it literally saves you from bankruptcy.

Budgeting your time is the same. It's the difference between having time for the things that matter—and, therefore, living the kind of life you want—and instead, spending your days slogging through an endless queue of tasks. So while I'm not saying you should spend hours a day constructing your Lego-based schedule, I *am* saying you should spend a few minutes on it—and that, in the long run, is time *very* well spent.

Indeed, there's a snowball effect. You start to develop better routines and habits; you start to find shortcuts. Maybe you save only a few minutes here and a few minutes there. But every forty-hour workweek is the sum of 480 five-minute segments. And as you continually manage your time better, and as you maintain better focus, you'll get more and more of those five-minute segments back—and they'll start to add up to hours, week in and week out. That will change your life.

Then come the psychological benefits.

We've all had those days where we feel like we've been working our butts off and have nothing to show for it. It's demoralizing, isn't it? On the other hand, we've *also* all had those days where we've accomplished so much we feel like Superman. Though every day can't be a Superman day, the more of those days that you can string together, the better you'll feel. In particular, **you'll feel the satisfaction of productivity and the lightness of leaving behind an unmanageable schedule. You'll build momentum and confidence in your ability to tackle your goals.**

As we explored way back in Chapter Two, the more excitement and passion you bring into each day, the better results you'll see.

We're good at things we're passionate about, and vice versa. It's a virtuous snowball effect that can keep rolling for years.

Now, all this talk of time management has put us on strong footing to answer our next—and very last—question:

How Do I Create Work-Life Balance as a Small-Business Owner?

There are few things more important than this question. And you could say this entire book has been building toward an answer. Take a second to consider the strategies we've covered.

On page one, we zoomed into the life of the typical small-business owner, who has collapsed from exhaustion after yet another dreary week of DIYing his entire business. From there, we considered **the million-dollar calculator**—the reason it's ludicrous for you to try to do everything yourself. There was **LeBron James and the reason he doesn't mow his own lawn** (among other reasons, because it's boring!). There was **the Golden Formula**, and the importance of focusing on your effective hourly rate, and increasing that rate all the time. There was honing your business model into *one thing* your business exists to do, and then doing that one thing better than anyone else; or, in other words, **do less, better**. We introduced the idea of the **small-business C-suite**, so that you have a team of experts quickly and efficiently dispatching the tasks that you previously tried to do all by yourself. There was the concept of **breaking up the value chain**, so your business can accomplish more while spending less. And there was a barrage of **digital tools** to help you automate or outsource tasks that just aren't cost-effective to do in-house.

> Imagine working 20 percent smarter instead of 20 percent longer. Work–life balance and start-up success at any stage aren't mutually exclusive. There are enough hours in the day to be effective and present.
>
> —David Cummings (Cofounder, Pardot)

Thanks to all of these strategies, the life of the small-business CEO looks very different than it did at the outset. You're running a smarter, sharper business with a crystal-clear value proposition and an expertly designed team to execute it. You sit at the helm of it all, your schedule no longer jammed with monotonous tasks that can be cost-effectively delegated. The value of your time has shot up; you're focused on adding as much value to your business as possible in each hour you work.

And with the **Focus + Lego-based Day Construction** approach to time management, you are ever clearer about what belongs on your plate and what doesn't. You're also better at delegating to your staff. In the past, you might not have been clear about what you expected your employees to accomplish and in what amount of time—since you weren't always clear about those things for yourself—but now you've changed all that. Using this new strategy for your own schedule has allowed you to become a better manager too.

You're also a lot clearer about your purpose in running your own business, and about your place in the world. **As an**

entrepreneur, you're helping your community pick more metaphorical apples off the metaphorical tree. In literal terms, you are *creating* wealth. And as an entrepreneur who creates wealth, not only for yourself but also for your family and the local—or even global—community, your time is extraordinarily valuable. The more time you spend on truly innovative, growth-obsessed, CEO-level thinking, the more value you're creating, and the virtuous cycle continues.

But achieving work–life balance—however you define it—means stepping back even from that larger perspective, and taking the time to consider where your business fits into your life priorities. Ask yourself:

How Do You Define Success?

It's a big question. Even more foundational than the question of *what's the **one thing** your business exists to do* is the question of *why do you want to start and run this business in the first place?*

In Part II we talked about "off-ramps," including the "lifestyle off-ramp," in which you choose not to grow your business beyond the size at which you can reasonably manage it yourself, as well as the "ultimate off-ramp," in which you achieve a level of financial success that allows you complete freedom in structuring your life. So, what's the ultimate goal for you?

Are you after the type of wild success that's measured in nine digits (or more) and which will require eighty hours a week for the next ten to twenty years to build? Great! Plan your time accordingly, using Lego-based Day Construction—and every other tool and strategy available to you—to make sure you use every minute of those eighty hours each week to their greatest potential.

But maybe you define success as *freedom*. The freedom to choose—whether to keep on working full-time at your business if you want to, or to put someone else in charge if you don't. Or the freedom to start a nonprofit, or to travel, or to spend more time with your family. And **if your priority is work–life balance—having time *now* to be with the people you love—then use that Lego-based Day Construction to build it into your daily life.**

But just as with time management, and just as with budgeting, you've got to have a plan. **Whatever your success looks like—whatever combination of financial reward, freedom, and time with loved ones—getting there requires articulating the big-picture end goal, and then mapping out your route for getting there. Starting *today*.**

And after this *Live Free or DIY* journey through international shipping, law firms, bagels, pizza shops, and the Digital Revolution, there's only one thing left to do: Put it all into action.

Epilogue: Time to Live Free

You don't have to make yourself miserable to be successful. It's natural to look back and mythologize the long nights and manic moments of genius, but success isn't about working hard; it's about working smart.

—Andrew Wilkinson

(Founder, MetaLab)

Whether your ultimate goal is wild financial success or more time with your family, achieving it means living free. Free to be your own boss. Free to choose your own path and to pursue your passion. Free to make a difference in the world. Free to leave a legacy for your children.

Yet there are a handful of roadblocks that small-business owners persistently identify as the problem areas that prevent them from achieving such freedom. You'll probably recognize at least a couple of them as challenges in your own business, and as topics to which this book has dedicated more than a few pages:

1. Getting and keeping customers;
2. Managing time and workload;
3. Managing resources, including funds and staff;
4. Dealing with red tape, from industry regulations to taxes; and
5. Low revenue.

When I set out to write this book, it was with the fundamental premise that none of these roadblocks is insurmountable. Though many small-business owners face a disheartening cycle of far too much monotonous work for far too little financial reward, the strategies and resources necessary for overcoming that cycle *are* out there. Hopefully, this book has instilled a sense of optimism by laying out, in no uncertain terms, a means for leaving behind that old way of doing things.

From escaping the DIY trap and building an expert outsourced C-suite, in Part I, to the Efficiency Roadmap and achieving the tightest possible product-market fit, in Part II, to adopting time-saving tools and adapting your workflow to the Digital Revolution, in Part III, to strategic management of time and money in Part IV, I hope that you've now got your sights on your own pathway to entrepreneurial success, and, more broadly, to financial and personal freedom.

But as this book's very title and each successive tool and tactic suggest, you can't do it alone. The efficiency of passion means you should do what you're passionate about—that's the reason you started your business, after all—and empower others to do what *they're* passionate about, in service to a great and well-honed business model focused on doing less, better. Your outsourced COO lives and breathes business operations. Your outsourced CFO's native language is budgets, spreadsheets, and KPIs. Your outsourced CHRO handles the ever-more-complex tangle of labor laws. And so on, all the way down to your frontline staff, however small, or part-time, or even virtual, that staff may be.

And **if you're ready to move toward this different way of running your small business, and if you'd like a little help in doing so, well, that help is out there.**

The same premise—and passion—that led me to write this book is exactly what's behind **Agents of Efficiency**, a business that exists for the sole purpose of serving as an outsourced COO for other small businesses. **If you want a partner in digging yourself out of the DIY trap and restructuring your back-office operations to make your business smarter, sharper, and more cost-effective—including identifying, hiring, and managing the rest of your small-business C-suite—then we're here for you.**

And I *don't* mean we're here just to tell you how to do it. As you now know, a COO should do *both* strategy and execution, and that's precisely what we do at Agents of Efficiency. We developed the Efficiency Roadmap to help you with strategy. But we also do the stuff you consider boring—the stuff that stands between you and that coveted freedom—so you can do what you're passionate about.

The results we help our clients achieve mean we become an additional source of profit for your business, not another expense. In fact, we guarantee an ROI in excess of our fee, or your money back!

To open a conversation about what this could look like for your business, get started at **WeDoBoring.com**.

But if you're not quite ready to take that leap just yet, head over to **LiveFree.WeDoBoring.com**, where you can sign up to get free access to a membership site we've setup exclusively for readers of this book. In it, you will find a ton of great resources from The Golden Formula Whitepaper, to The Digital Business Model Canvas Template, to an Expense Tracker, to access to an otherwise paid course on Growth Hacking. It's full of a wealth of tools and resources to help you dig deeper into some of the concepts introduced in this book.

And regardless of whether or not you're seeking a partner in making these changes to the way you do business, I wish you all the luck. May you truly live free!

Endnotes

Chapter 1

1. Elaine Pofeldt, "U.S. Entrepreneurship Hits Record High," Forbes, 27 May 2013, http://www.forbes.com/sites/elainepofeldt/2013/05/27/u-s-entrepreneurship-hits-record-high/.
2. Stanford, The Relationship Between Hours Worked and Productivity," http://cs.stanford.edu/people/eroberts/cs181/projects/crunchmode/econ-hours-productivity.html.

Chapter 2

3. "Am I Boring You?," narrated by Stephen J. Dubner, Freakonomics, 29 October 2015, http://freakonomics.com/2015/10/29/am-i-boring-you-a-new-freakonomics-radio-episode/.
4. David A. Vise and Mark Malseed, The Google Story: For Google's 10th Birthday, Delta, 2008. E-book.

Chapter 3

5. Neil Patel, "90% of Startups Fail; Here's What You Need to Know About the 10%," Forbes, 16 Jan. 2015, http://www.forbes.com/sites/neilpatel/2015/01/16/90-of-startups-will-fail-heres-what-you-need-to-know-about-the-10/.

6. Eric T. Wagner, "Five Reasons 8 out of 10 Businesses Fail," Forbes, 12 Sept. 2013, http://www.forbes.com/sites/ericwagner/2013/09/12/five-reasons-8-out-of-10-businesses-fail/.

Chapter 4

7. AIMM Consulting, "A Financial Case for Employment Testing," http://www.aimmconsult.com/AFinancialCaseforAssessment.pdf.

8. Ruben Melendez and Colin Rice, "Outsourcing ROI," Industry Week, 9 June 2008, http://www.industryweek.com/companies-amp-executives/outsourcing-roi.

9. "Hyperactive, yet passive," *The Economist*, 5 Dec. 2015, http://www.economist.com/news/leaders/21679450-worries-about-corporate-myopia-miss-point-even-america-business-not-dynamic.

10. Margaret Haynes, "Rethinking Outsourcing in Light of Economic Conditions," First Data Corporation White Paper, May 2009, https://www.firstdata.com/downloads/thought-leadership/fd_rethinkingoutsourcing_whitepaper.pdf.

11. Based on the Intuit Small Business Employment Index, which found that, since 2010, employment growth among PEO clients has been 9 percent higher than other small businesses, and 4 percent higher than employment growth in the US economy overall.

12. Research by the Society of Human Resources Management, 2002, as cited by the National Association of Professional Employer Organizations.

13. "National client e-mail report 2015," The Direct Marketing Association (UK) LTD, 2015, http://cdn.emailmonday.com/wp-content/uploads/2015/04/National-client-email-2015-DMA.pdf.

Chapter 6:

14. "The Restaurant Failure Myth," *Bloomberg Business*, 16 April 2007, http://www.bloomberg.com/bw/stories/2007-04-16/the-restaurant-failure-mythbusinessweek-business-news-stock-market-and-financial-advice.

Chapter 9:

15. Randall Stross, "Feeling Like a Buggy Whip Maker? Better Check Your Simile," The New York Times, 9 Jan. 2010, http://www.nytimes.com/2010/01/10/business/10digi.html?_r=1.

Chapter 12:

16. Renzulli, Linda A. and Howard Aldrich, "Who Can You Turn to? Tie Activation within Core Business Discussion Networks," *Social Forces*, 84.1 (Sept. 2005): 323-341.

17. Dulsrud, Arne and Kjel Grønhaug, "Is Friendship Consistent with Competitive Market Exchange? A Microsociological Analysis of the Fish Export-Import Business," *Acta Sociologica*, 50.1 (March 2007): 7-19.

18. Minkoff, Debra C, "Producing Social Capital," *American Behavioral Scientist*, 40:5 (1997): 606-619.

19. Wellman, Barry, "Structural Analysis: From method and metaphor to theory and substance," *Social Structures a Network Approach*, New York: Cambridge University Press, 1988.

Chapter 15:

20. Ken Makovsky, "Where Customer Service Doesn't Matter," *Forbes*, 23 Jan. 2014, http://www.forbes.com/sites/kenmakovsky/2014/01/23/where-customer-service-doesnt-matter/.

21. Neil Patel, "How To Make More Money Without Making More Sales," *Forbes*, 17 Nov. 2014, http://www.forbes.com/sites/neilpatel/2014/11/17/how-to-make-more-money-without-making-more-sales/.

22. Jerry Jao, "Customer Retention Should Outweigh Customer Acquisition," CMO, 2 Aug. 2013, http://www.cmo.com/articles/2013/7/18/customer_retention.html.

23. Neil Patel, "How To Make More Money Without Making More Sales," *Forbes*, 17 Nov. 2014, http://www.forbes.com/sites/neilpatel/2014/11/17/how-to-make-more-money-without-making-more-sales/.
24. Amy Gallo, "The Value of Keeping the Right Customers," Harvard Business Review, 29 Oct. 2014, https://hbr.org/2014/10/the-value-of-keeping-the-right-customers/.

CPSIA information can be obtained at www.ICGtesting.com
Printed in the USA
BVOW06*0302090716

454816BV00002B/2/P

9 780692 671238